SPEAK
& MEET
VIRTUALLY

Go from Zoom Fatigue, Online Meeting Boredom, and Impersonal Presentations to Engaging, Efficient, and Empowering Web Conferencing

MIKE ACKER

Copyright ©2021, Mike Acker

All rights reserved. No part of this publication may be reproduced, distributed, or transmitted in any form or by any means, including photocopying, recording, or other electronic or mechanical methods, without the prior written permission of the publisher, except in the case of brief quotations embodied in reviews and certain other non-commercial uses permitted by copyright law.

Some names and identifying details have been changed to protect the privacy of individuals.

ISBN: 978-1-954024-22-9 Paperback
        978-1-954024-23-6 Hardcover
        978-1-954024-24-3 Ebook

        https://www.advantage-publishing.com

    To contact, please e-mail: contact@mikeacker.com

READ FIRST

Thank you for investing in my book.
As an appreciation, I'd love to give you a free gift.

Communication Coaching Videos

These cover the "3 Classics" that are the basis of effective public speaking and the "3 Questions" that will help you write better speeches.

These are the foundation of my coaching and have helped hundreds of people gain clarity and direction in creating their speech. In addition, there are many great resources related to the content of this book at https://content.mikeacker.com

Visit the link or use the QR code for your gift:

CONTENTS

"To boldly go where no one has gone before."

Star Trek

INTRODUCTION

In 1966, *Star Trek* kicked off an era of sci-fi wonder. We saw Captain James T. Kirk sit confidently in his seat, talking to other races lightyears away. Technology allowed them to virtually zoom across the galaxy to discuss treaties, alliances, and commerce—without even engaging warp drive.

Star Trek made it look glamorous. What if we could sit in our office and talk to anyone, anywhere—wouldn't that be amazing? Can you imagine if we had technology that operated like a window to anywhere in the world?

Then, like *Star Trek's* automatic doors and cell phones (communicators), another sci-fi dream became a reality.:

- Cisco launched WebEx in 1995.

- Zoom started in 2011.

- Microsoft Teams was introduced in 2017.

Since the dawn of this web conference era, we have learned that it can indeed be amazing to zoom anywhere in the world: office complexes, homes, classrooms, cars, dining rooms, TV talk shows, and (unfortunately) even bathrooms.

With the COVID-19 pandemic of 2020, virtual communication platforms, such as Zoom, flew through the "Early Adoption" phase and straight to "Late Majority":

- 27% of small businesses used web conferencing.

- 43% of remote and in-house teams used web conferencing.

- 83% of businesses with over 250 employees used some form of virtual communication.

As of the time of this writing, an unbelievable 11 million virtual meetings are being held every *day*, allowing for unprecedented interaction across the world. But...

- 44% of professionals surveyed said they've experienced video call fatigue since the start of the pandemic.

- 59% said video calls can be helpful but are not always necessary.

- 22% said that the practicality and novelty of video conferencing has worn off over the past eight months. [1]

In another survey, 69% of participants said virtual meetings have become an obstacle and another study revealed that 37% of these meetings are extremely ineffective. Altogether, modern-day Zoomers consistently express frustration, disconnection, and burnout. 2020 even coined the term: Zoom fatigue.

---

[1] https://www.roberthalf.ca/en/44-of-workers-are-suffering-from-video-call-fatigue-robert-half-research-shows

Sound familiar? Do you cringe every time you receive a Zoom invite and sigh with relief when you click "End Meeting for All"? Or maybe you don't mind virtual meetings, but wished your team was more present in their meetings.

Whether you think online meetings are a blessing or curse (or a mixture of the two), you probably got this book because you believe that they can be done *better*. I'm here to tell you, you're right. Done correctly, virtual communication can be the marvel *Star Trek* promised. Consider:

- 87% of remote team members say that they feel more connected to their colleagues with video conferencing.[2]

- 90% of respondents believe that video makes it easier for them to get their point across.[3]

- 89% of respondents say that video conferencing reduces the time required to complete projects or tasks.[4]

- 94% of businesses believe access to video conferencing improves their productivity.[5]

The purpose of this book is to show how you and your company can maximize the benefits of virtual communication while minimizing the disadvantages. It isn't a user manual for Skype nor will I teach you the top ten shortcuts for Zoom. It's

---

[2] https://gigaom.com/report/why-videoconferencing-is-critical-to-business-collaboration/
[3] https://www.lifesize.com/en/video-conferencing-blog/productivity-results-are-in
[4] Ibid.
[5] https://www.slideshare.net/bluejeannw/10-must-know-video-conferencing-stats

all about being a great communicator and leading amazing meetings, regardless of the specific platform.

(If you are just looking for a PDF to give you some basic tips and some recommended resources, go to:

https://subscribe.stepstoadvance.com/virtual)

Maximize the benefits of virtual communication while minimizing the drawbacks.

As an executive and communication coach who works with clients around the world, I was using video conferencing long before COVID made it "cool." As a result, I learned early on how to adapt the communication principles that I regularly taught for *virtual* communication platforms.

Five days each week, I work at the computer, sometimes spending as much as *ten hours* on Zoom. But when I'm done, I'm able to unplug and rush out, invigorated and ready to play with my son and help my wife with dinner. I know, from experience, that virtual communication doesn't have to leave you drained and disconnected. It has the power to energize you, create greater connections, and improve your team's effectiveness.

When my son was three years old, I began that rite of passage: teaching him to use a public restroom on his own. My son would go inside while I stood outside and coached him. I had to talk loudly through the frosted glass, asking, "Son, you alright in there?" as I wondered if he'd fallen in. "Do you need help? Oh, and make sure to wash your hands!"

It had been simpler and taken less time when he was smaller, and I was there in person. Now the door created a barrier, a solid obstacle I had to work through. Talking through the door took awareness, targeted energy, and intentionality. But now, he's fully trained, and I don't even have to leave my seat!

Virtual communication, likewise, creates both an obstacle and an opportunity and, by taking the extra effort to learn how to effectively "talk through the door," we can create a system that works better for everyone.

Virtual communication creates both an obstacle and an opportunity.

Throughout this book, I will teach you how to become a pro at virtual meetings and how to train others to become more proficient. Like talking through the bathroom door to my son, this will require intentionality and extra effort at the front end, but the payoff will be huge as your virtual meetings become engaging, efficient, and enjoyable.

You will likely find yourself becoming a more confident leader and speaker in the process.

My promise to you is that this book will be high on impact and low on fluff. Everything in here is designed to build your skills, not fill pages. I wrote it to be a quick, practical guide that will have a measurable impact by the end of the first chapter.

So, here's the game plan. There are four sections in this book:

1. *Engaging:* How to effectively connect with the other participants as people, not pictures on a screen.

2. *Attending:* How to get and give the most as a participant in virtual meetings.

3. *Leading:* How to lead great meetings that people will *want* to attend.

4. *Setting Up:* How to prepare your equipment and "virtual office space" for maximum impact.

Why does "Setting Up" come at the end? Because it's largely the technical content and I wanted to dive into the actionable content immediately! Along the way, I'll include some bonus tips:

- *60 Second Fixes:* Quick changes you can make immediately to improve your virtual communication.

- *Virtual Opportunity:* Under-appreciated advantages of online communication.

- *Ergo-tips*: Practical advice that helps both your body and your communication.

Unsure if you want to invest your energy and time into this book?

When I was 23 years old, I decided to enroll in the Dale Carnegie Institute. It was an investment of several thousand dollars that I didn't really have. But, as I looked at my goals, I knew I needed to invest in my communication skills and believed that my investment would pay off. And it has—many,

many times over. The skills I learned landed me jobs, made me more effective, and taught me the value of professional advancement. Communication skills translate into currency.

Communication skills translate into currency.

As I said, COVID-19 catapulted the world into the virtual communication age. The lockdowns may or may not be over, but things are not ever going back to the way they were. The new normal includes workers that expect greater flexibility, changing modes of interactions, and the decline of geographical limitations.

This has created a unique opportunity for those individuals and companies willing to invest in upping their game:

Companies that embrace the new normal will gain a competitive edge over those who don't, especially as they are able to attract and retain talent uninterested in the old desk and cubicle routine.

Individuals who invest in excelling at virtual communication will stand out against the multitudes satisfied with mediocrity. It's still not too late to become a "Zoom rock star."

Turn the page and let's get started—don't waste another minute in ineffective and impersonal virtual meetings!

PART ONE: ENGAGE

Effective online communication requires engaging a person,
not a computer.

Chapter 1:
Change Perspective

Think about the words "engage" and "engagement."

Engagement may be a noun, but it's still an active word, indicating movement. Whether we're talking about a personal or business engagement, it is something you *do*. It takes effort.

Engage is a transitive verb. I know grammar was a long time ago for many of us, but that means it requires an object. In other words, it is directed *to* someone or something. We get engaged to someone, an army engages an enemy, a good book or movie engages you, we engage people in conversation.

Effective online communication requires engaging a person, not a computer.

Effective online communication requires engaging a person not a computer. I cannot stress this enough. It's key to bringing excellence to webinars, web conferences, and online meetings—whether you're the presenter or an attender. It's vital never to forget that you are talking to real people and to engage them as if they were really there.

Intellectually, that seems obvious, but most people act like they're talking to a computer, not a person. Virtual engagement requires an act of imagination. You have to *pretend* that the camera is a real person (notice I said camera, not screen—we'll get back to that shortly).

Virtual engagement requires an act of imagination.

SOCIAL VS. SOLO

Imagine a meeting in the boardroom. Make the room as stereotypical as you can. See the long oak table and black executive chairs running along both sides. To your right, floor to ceiling windows that look out upon the city from high above. Now add the CEO in her seat at the head of the table and the rest of the top execs, all dressed very professionally.

How would you prepare for that meeting? Would you have your presentation well-honed, all your materials organized, and thought through every possible question and your response? How would you dress? Would you feel a thrill of fear as you walked through the door?

Now imagine sitting down to your computer in the privacy of your bedroom, with your kids watching TV in the living room, and writing an email to that same CEO. Would you dress up in your most professional clothes? Would you feel the same fear as when you clicked "New Email"?

Of course, you wouldn't.

Working on a computer is inherently a solo activity and meetings are a social activity. What I mean is that we're always in one of two modes: solo and social. Solo doesn't have to mean being by yourself. If you're at home on a Saturday morning with your spouse or a longtime roommate, you're probably still in solo mode—you don't care about unbrushed teeth or well-worn sweatpants and college t-shirts.

Working on a computer is inherently a solo activity while meetings are a social activity.

Another way to describe it is *on stage* versus *offstage*. When you're in solo mode, you don't take into account how others see you. If, on that same Saturday, you got a call from your new neighbors asking to borrow sugar, you'll probably brush your teeth, put on nice sweatpants, and make sure the view from the front door is acceptable. What's happened? You've switched into social mode.

Before the pandemic, in-person meetings activated your social mode. Even if you're an introvert, you still rose to the social challenge. You dressed for the occasion, shook hands, smiled, and made small talk. More importantly, you leaned in to listen, nodded your head, looked people in the eye, maintained correct posture, and worked on being fully present.

Those actions took more effort than tapping away on a keyboard, but you were rewarded with human connection, dynamic feedback, and emotional energy.

However, once you left the meeting and sat down at your computer, you switched back to solo mode. Your brain turned off the need to read social cues and shifted that capacity to the work at hand. We inherently view computer work as solo work.

We inherently view computer work as solo work.

I asked you to first imagine a boardroom meeting and then drafting an email. Now imagine a third scenario: You're about to attend a virtual meeting with your CEO and give a presentation. You'll still be alone in your bedroom, but now you'll be interacting with real people.

Will you be in social mode or solo mode?

If you're like most people, you'll be in solo mode. Don't believe me? In "real" meetings, we…

- … maintain appropriate eye contact.

- … don't hide behind a black piece of paper with our name on it (i.e., turn the camera off).

- … pay attention to our posture and what it communicates.

- … don't overtly surf the web.

- … offer real-time feedback.

- … don't forget to wear our pants.

The central obstacle to excellence in virtual communication is that we inherently treat it like computer-work instead of people-work. Our focus is more on "virtual" than "communication" and connection.

We treat virtual communication like computer-work instead of people-work.

Think back to Captain James T. Kirk on his intergalactic Zoom call. He stayed in an active social mode instead of a passive solo mode. He didn't multitask but fully engaged his audience. He maintained a posture of command and interest. He dressed in his uniform, signifying to his audience (and his own psyche) that he was in work mode. He maintained vocal variety and spoke with slightly increased volume. He engaged the images on the screen as if they were people, not computers.

To gain greater connection and effectiveness via virtual meetings, we must change our perspective and see them like the social events they are. We need to treat virtual conversations like real conversations. We have to engage the people on the other side of the camera.

Treat virtual conversations like real conversations.

60 Second Fix

In your next virtual meeting, remind yourself to stay in social mode by imagining that you're being watched on a huge, hi-def screen. Every time you glance away from the screen (and down at your phone), they'll know. Every time you get distracted or daze out, it will be as obvious as if you were there in person.

Returning to how I taught my son to use the restroom while speaking through a closed door, I want to remind you that virtual communication creates new challenges, provides new opportunities, and requires new skills. Meeting with a person that isn't actually present creates an obstacle but—done right—it can be a game-changer.

Effective virtual communication requires intentionality.

Chapter 2:
Virtual Connection

As I write this, the COVID lockdowns have largely been lifted, but memories of painful separation are still fresh: Grandparents in care facilities unable to receive visitors, couples unable to cross the international borders, friends unable to gather for their traditional game night, and children in cancer wards unable to see extended family.

To all these people, video chats seemed like a miracle. Even though physically separated, they were able to be connected virtually—as Facebook liked to remind us via heart-touching commercials.

The most obvious advantage of virtual communication is that it allows connection where otherwise it would be impractical or impossible. In one survey, 89% of people said video conferencing helps them to feel connected to the people they care about and an amazing 98% said it strengthens relationships both outside and inside the company.[6] This technology especially benefits remote team members who used to feel left out of the company's culture.

---

[6] https://www.lifesize.com/en/blog/productivity-results-are-in/

Virtual Opportunity

It used to be that geography was a significant obstacle to finding clients and connecting with leaders in your field. As people become increasingly comfortable with virtual communication, geography is less of a limitation. Obviously, it's no substitute for rubbing elbows at a conference, but don't let that stop you from taking advantage of the new opportunities.

It's easy to blame our fatigue on web conferencing, saying, "It's just not personal" or "I don't feel engaged." But the problem isn't the medium—it's how we are using it.

My wife and I first met at a conference in Atlanta, which was where she lived at the time. After the conference was over, I returned to the Seattle area. While we could have called each other, MySpace was really how we connected—that tells you how long ago it was! After I'd sent off a message on MySpace, I didn't sigh with relief and complain about how impersonal it was. I was energized and grateful for the opportunity to connect in a somewhat personal way.

When two people invest their energy into any relationship, they are rewarded with positive results. That energy then supplies new energy to the relationship. However, if either one of them starts devoting less energy, the relationship deteriorates and begins to drain both people, often resulting in disconnection.

The same is true in web conferencing. Less energy given results in less energy. But increased effort in virtual communication will make you more energized, more connected, and ultimately more effective.

The more energy you give to virtual communication, the more you will receive.

---

60 Second Fix

Before your next virtual meeting, give yourself a pep talk. Shift your attitude towards the positive. Prepared to give it your full attention and expect to get energy from it.

TALKING THROUGH THE DOOR

Obviously, virtual meetings are not the same as in-person meetings. In the same way that talking to my son through the restroom door required intentionality, effective virtual engagement requires specific skills. I was talking to a bartender friend about working during the pandemic and he said that the greatest challenge was learning to engage his customers through a face mask. So much of bartending is personal interaction and facial expressions are key to connecting.

He intentionally worked to overcome these challenges by learning to smile extra big, allowing them to see the smile in his eyes and hear it in his voice (did you know that the best call centers teach their representatives to smile as they talk to you?). He also avoided teasing his clients because the risk of being misunderstood was much higher without facial clues. Finally, he spoke louder and more distinctly and used his hands more.

Why did he make such an effort to engage his customers? Because his ability to connect directly impacted his tips. Communication translates into currency.

Virtual communication faces many of the same challenges. As I've said before, it creates a barrier between you and the other participants. Let's talk about how to "speak through" that barrier.

The greater the physical distance between you and your audience, the bigger you need to be.

As a public speaking coach, I frequently remind my clients to act natural *plus some* when on stage—a speaker needs to adopt an exaggerated model of self. The greater the physical distance between you and your audience, the bigger you need to be.

In the same way, effective virtual communication must be exaggerated slightly to be seen and heard the way you want to be. It's much more like acting in a play than a movie—there are no close-up angles to capture your minute facial expressions.

Because we inherently approach computer work in solo mode, most people tend to become less animated, talk more quietly, and lean away from the computer. This is the opposite of what you need to do. You need to increase your excitement, lean into the computer, and work harder to engage your audience.

Does this kind of engagement require more energy? Absolutely. But, in return, your audience becomes more energetic and then returns that energy to you.

---

60 Second Fix

The next time you have to give a virtual presentation, find a way to raise your computer to "standing eye level" (I've been known to use books and even hotel ottomans when traveling) and give your presentation standing up. You will immediately feel more energy and power. We'll talk a little more about this in Chapter 12.

ACTIVE LISTENING

Have you ever poured out your soul to someone only to have them say, "I'm sorry, what was that? I wasn't listening." Or have you tried to have a serious conversation with someone as they kept glancing at their cell phone?

Good communication isn't just about the speaker—it's also about the listener. As a participant in a virtual meeting, you are a key contributor and the way you listen, or fail to listen, will directly impact the speaker and therefore the quality of the presentation.

The way you listen, or fail to listen, impacts the quality of the meeting.

Remember our mindset: virtual meetings are social, not solo, activities. Be present whether you're talking *or* listening. Think of how you demonstrate interest in face-to-face meetings:

- Lean in closer for a key point.

- Nod to indicate agreement.

- Lean back and fold arms or shake your head to disagree.

- Smile to encourage.

- Maintain eye contact.

- Interject "listening noises."

- Ask questions when you need clarity.

This is basic Golden Rule stuff—treat others the way you want to be treated.

DISTRACTED & DISTRACTIONS

One survey showed that 20% of respondents believed that virtual meetings were "rarely productive" and that almost half preferred face-to-face meetings. But more than 50% of those surveyed admitted to not giving their full attention to the meeting. Instead, they were:

- Checking email.

- Texting.

- Multitasking.

- Snacking.

- Scrolling through social media.

- Surfing the internet.

- Doing household chores.

- Playing video games.[7]

The survey didn't specifically say so, but I bet that 100% of the 20% who called virtual meetings unproductive were part of the 50% that were distracted! (Did you follow all that...)

---

[7] https://www.zippia.com/advice/virtual-meetings-zoom-survey/

Virtual Opportunity

According to one survey, 82% of people are less likely to multitask on a video call than a phone call.[8] I think the reason is twofold. First, the video feed keeps them more engaged. Second, they're more likely to get caught!

It's easy to blame inefficiency on poorly run meetings—for good reasons. The effectiveness of meetings rises and falls on the skills of the facilitators, and we'll discuss that in depth in Part Three. But distracted participants share in the blame. If half of them are visibly distracted (you're never hiding it as well as you think), it both demoralizes the presenter and encourages everyone else to check out. As participation plummets, so does effectiveness.

Oh, and multitasking is a myth. Our brains don't actually do tasks simultaneously. They switch rapidly between tasks, such as listening to a podcast and typing an email, but lose some efficiency with each switch.[9] So, as my editor, Josh Kelley, likes to say, "Multitasking is just a great way to be a 'half-ass-king.'"

Multitasking is just a great way to be a "half-ass-king."

---

[8] https://www.lifesize.com/en/blog/productivity-results-are-in/
[9] https://www.psychologytoday.com/us/blog/creativity-without-borders/201405/the-myth-multitasking

In addition to distracted participants, unexpected *distractions* are a common problem in web conferences. Zoom fails that have gone viral include playful cats, intruding toddlers, and less-than-discreet bathrooms. These may be hilarious in someone else's meeting, but not yours. Take the necessary precautions to avoid trending on YouTube for the wrong reasons.

INTENTIONALITY

The key to this chapter is *intentionality*. The parent talking through the bathroom door, the bartender communicating through a face mask, and the rock star Zoomer all have this in common: they are incredibly intentional about the way they communicate, paying attention both to how they speak and how they listen. Their short-term efforts are rewarded with long term results.

Effective virtual communication requires intentionality.

———————————

For most people, eye contact is the single most crucial element of communication. Virtual communication complicates eye contact on many levels, from where to look to combatting eye strain. That's our next topic.

Treat the camera like the eyes of a real person.

Chapter 3:
It's All in the Eyes

"The eyes are the window of the soul."

You've heard that a thousand times. The expression has been around since Shakespeare, but the concept is much, much older. As far back as the 1st century BCE, Cicero said, "The face is a picture of the mind as the eyes are its interpreter."

Science only continues to back this up. You can fake a smile or feign interest, but you have no voluntary control over your pupils and they give others insight into what you really feel.[10] We are highly attuned to the smallest detail of someone else's eyes. Have you noticed that you can tell if a pedestrian is looking at you, even if their head doesn't move and you pass them at 60 MPH?

Virtual engagement requires paying special attention to your eyes. It also requires taking good care of your eyes because extended screen time is a major cause of mental fatigue. Fortunately, the "eye solutions" are surprisingly simple.

---

[10] https://www.psychologytoday.com/us/blog/talking-apes/201512/your-eyes-really-are-the-window-your-soul

Virtual engagement requires paying
special attention to your eyes.

LOOK AT THE CAMERA

The first "eye fix" may be the most important principle in the whole book, and it's certainly the simplest: Treat the camera like the eyes of the other participants. You probably already know this from taking selfies. If you focus on your image on the phone, you appear to be looking down. It's only when you're looking at the camera that you appear to be looking straight ahead.

Treat the camera like the eyes of a real person.

It works the exact same way in virtual meetings. If you look at the speaker or gallery (or yourself), you'll appear to be looking away from them. This is where the principle "Virtual engagement requires an act of imagination" comes into play. You have to pretend that the camera is the audience's eyes. The good news is that it gets easier with practice, as any TV reporter can tell you.

CAMERA PLACEMENT

The second eye fix is almost as easy: place the camera at eye level. This can be done by either using an external camera on a stand or raising up your computer (I'll talk more about equipment in Chapter 12). Raising the camera and focusing on it instead of the screen has several immediate benefits:

60 Second Fix

Position your camera—not screen—at eye level and learn to focus on *it* whenever you are speaking. It's a simple fix that will make a significant impact. Remember, virtual communication is a social activity, so you must engage the camera as if it were a real person.

1. CREATES CONNECTION

When you look into the camera, you are effectively making eye contact and shifting from solo mode to social mode. On an interpersonal level, eye contact is vital for communication. For instance, your brain subtly processes the dilation in the other person's pupils, telling you that they are interested in what you're saying.

When you look into the camera, you shift from solo mode to social mode.

On a physiological level, eye contact has long been understood to be valuable, with studies showing that prolonged eye contact releases phenylethylamine, a chemical associated with feelings of attraction. In workplaces, you aren't necessarily looking for phenylethylamine, but you are looking for connection. This connection energizes you and encourages you to continue communicating.

Obviously, you can't have actual two-way eye contact in virtual meetings. When you're looking into the camera, you can't look in the other person's eyes and visa-versa. It's kind of like the difference between using a telephone and a walkie-talkie. On a telephone, you both can talk at the same time, but on a walkie-talkie, you take turns. In virtual meetings, emotionally rewarding eye contact requires taking turns looking at the camera and looking at the person.

Virtual Opportunity
When I was starting out as a public speaker, I had to intentionally move my eyes from person to person and remember not to stare at one person for too long. In virtual meetings, it's much simpler. By focusing on the camera, you get to make contact with everyone without them worrying that they have something stuck in their teeth!

2. PROVIDES FOCUS

In leading many virtual workshops and coaching well over 500 individuals in 2020, I observed that most Zoomers now know how to unmute and mute but don't know where to look or how to hold themselves.

They are making it too complicated. As I said, when you imagine that the other person is physically present and that the camera is their eyes, you'll naturally know where to look and how to hold yourself.

This act of imagination also makes it easier to know how much "eye contact" to make. In everyday conversations, staring feels aggressive. Avoiding eye contact communicates passiveness or that you're uncomfortable. But the right amount of eye contact conveys interest and friendliness.[11]

The right amount of eye contact conveys interest and friendliness.

Don't *stare* at the camera, any more than you'd stare into someone's eyes for an entire meeting. Occasionally, glance to the side when you're thinking. Let your eyes flit around the screen to check in on your own posture and setup. But always keep coming back to their "eyes."

---

60 Second Fix

Attend your next virtual meetings in "gallery mode" and arrange the feeds so that you and the main speaker are just below your camera. There are two reasons for this.

First, having another person on full screen makes them feel uncomfortably close to you. Professor Jeremy Bailenson, founding director of the Stanford Virtual Human Interaction Lab, says that excessive close-up eye contact is very intense and emotionally draining.[12] Beyond the emotional toll,

---

[11] https://www.everydayhealth.com/healthy-living/eye-contact-what-you-need-know/
[12] Ibid

it pulls your eyes to the center of the screen and away from the camera.

Second, it allows you to focus on the camera while watching the others out of the corner of your eye. Why keep yourself at the top? Because human nature compels you to look at yourself, so don't make it obvious by having your image at the bottom of the screen!

On the other hand, Bailenson believes that watching yourself in real time is fatiguing and suggests using the "Hide self-view" option.[13] Try both ways and see what works best for you.

It's important to note that eye contact is perceived differently from culture to culture. Americans see eye contact as a sign of honesty (hence the expression "He won't look me in the eyes"). But in many cultures, it's seen as aggressive or disrespectful. Even two linguistically related countries, like America and Britain, will have different norms.[14] If you are going to communicate with someone from a different culture, research how they view eye contact and adjust accordingly.

---

[13] https://news.stanford.edu/2021/02/23/four-causes-zoom-fatigue-solutions/
[14] https://techfeatured.com/10604/eye-contact-in-different-cultures

3. LOOKS BETTER

Positioning the camera at eye level both prevents you from (literally) looking down on everyone else, and it also makes you look better—there's a reason people don't take selfies from below eye level! Eye level is more flattering. Try a quick experiment: Take one snapshot from your normal setup and then another with your computer's camera at eye level. Share both on social media and see which one is more popular.

Eye level is more flattering.

4. REDUCES FATIGUE

Staring at the screen drains us as our eyes constantly focus and refocus. Eyes struggle to shift from the bright center of characters and shapes to the pixels' softer edges.

Like carpal tunnel syndrome, when our eyes run the same micro-pattern repeatedly, it strains our eyes and mind. This results in CVS. Not the pharmacy, but "Computer Vision Syndrome." Symptoms include headaches, blurred vision, neck pain, fatigue, and irritated eyes.[15] According to doctors, it only gets worse as you get older. Yay...

By looking at the camera, you allow your eyes to focus on something that is fixed, giving them a break. Using an external camera increases this benefit.

---

[15] https://en.wikipedia.org/wiki/Computer_vision_syndrome

60 Second Fix

Another contributor to CVS is tension from focusing on a close object for long periods of time. Ophthalmologists suggest the '20-20-20' rule: Every 20 minutes, take a 20-second break and look at something 20 feet away.[16]

5. LESS STRAIN ON NECK

Putting your camera at eye level isn't just about better communication—it's less strain on your neck.

After injuring my neck in a car accident, I needed some chiropractic care. My doctor pointed to the analogy of holding a bowling ball. When bowling, we naturally hold the ball close to our chest because the closer it is, the lighter it feels. The chiropractor explained that the head is like a ten-pound bowling ball on top of your neck. Every inch you lean forward effectively adds an extra 10 pounds of weight for your neck to carry. Hence, looking down at the screen of a laptop or a camera increases the force of torque, wearing you out physically through the course of the day.

---

[16] https://web.archive.org/web/20171008031120/http://health.economictimes.indiatimes.com/news/diagnostics/millions-at-risk-of-computer-vision-syndrome/52515980

To sum up the first three chapters, effective virtual communication requires embracing it as a social activity and being just as engaged as you would be in a face-to-face meeting yet making key adjustments to overcome its barriers.

It's great to be engaged, but you also want to accomplish something. In the next two sections, we're going to focus on *preparing for*, and *being in* the meetings. First, we'll focus on your role as a participant because how you prepare and what you do in the meeting doesn't just affect you. You can make everyone's experience much better or... much worse.

PART TWO: **PREPARATION**

There's nothing better than coming into a meeting
at the top of your game.

Chapter 4:
Get Ready

Thomas Sowell once wrote, "People who enjoy meetings should not be in charge of anything." Given the number of pointless, meeting-for-the-sake-of-meeting meetings I've attended (and, unfortunately, led), I understand the sentiment. But I've also been a part of some amazing meetings that created insightful discussion and led to decisive action. As the ancient King Solomon said, "Without counsel plans fail, but with many advisers they succeed."[17]

What makes the difference between an effective and ineffective meeting?

Two things: people and preparation. Good meetings require the right people prepared to meet, being led by someone who is also prepared to facilitate the meeting. This chapter focuses on getting yourself ready for a great meeting. It focuses on the participants, but much of it will apply to the facilitators as well. Much of it may seem like common sense, but the virtual age has made us sloppier, literally, and figuratively!

---

[17] Proverbs 15:22 (ESV).

DRESSED FOR SUCCESS

I was talking to another coach about a recent single-session client. As always, she prepared for their session by going through her notes and dressing professionally for their Zoom meeting. Throughout the meeting, the client kept the camera uptight to his face. It didn't create a really flattering view, but she just ignored it. As he'd move around, the camera angle would shift and she finally realized that he was still in bed and wasn't even wearing a shirt! Obviously, that was incredibly unprofessional, but he was the client, so she finished their session without comment.

Here's what I found so interesting. She almost always gets five-star reviews, but this client gave her a rare four stars. But I know that she gave him the same high-quality coaching she always gives. I believe that it was his lack of preparation and professionality that made him incapable of receiving the full value of her work.

How you dress matters. You and I both know that.

I'm a speaker coach for Seattle TEDx. This is a very professional group. Almost all of them have several advanced degrees and are leaders in their field. When I work with them, I dress to represent myself in a very professional manner, wearing a sports coat and dress shoes at a minimum. I'm sure you've been in a similar situation and know how much appearance affects how people react to you. Maybe you've hired a stylist to help you improve your fashion sense. Even "business casual" is more complicated than your Saturday morning clothes. Your appearance communicates volumes.

Then the COVID pandemic completely upended normal life. It forced most of us to work from home and we struggled to adjust as virtual meetings became the norm. In those chaotic days, we seemed to forget everything we knew about dressing for success. A lot of that was driven by the rapid changes and the massive emotional strain we were under. But, as virtual communication becomes the new normal, it's vital to remember that your *virtual* appearance also communicates volumes.

Your virtual appearance communicates volumes.

As that shirtless client demonstrated, dressing for success isn't just about what it communicates to others. It affects how we *feel* about ourselves—we all know that feeling of putting on our most professional outfit. But during the COVID lockdown, the pants sales dropped, shirts sales increased, and pajamas sky-rocketed. Business attire on top and sweatpants (or worse) on bottom become the norm. It may be more comfortable, but it can still negatively impact productivity.

Even if you don't slip up and accidentally show your under-pants, as some Zoomers have done, only dressing for the camera will negatively impact you. As Dawnn Karen, author of *Dress Your Best Life*, said, "If you're not able to [or choose not to!] wear your outfit that you wear to work, you feel less productive. You feel useless. That affects your self-esteem."[18]

---

[18] https://www.washingtonpost.com/business/2020/03/28/walmart-coronavirus-shirts-pants/

I'm not saying that you need to dress all the way up for every web conference. I usually wear slippers for Zoom meetings— our home is a "take your shoes off at the door" house—but when I'm doing a virtual keynote speech, I still wear dress shoes. It makes a difference in how I feel. So, experiment, and find out what works best for you. Do you feel at the top of your game when you're dressed professionally from head to toe, or can you be a little more casual?

ARRIVE EARLY AND PREPARE YOUR SPACE

Other than not wearing pants, few things are less professional than making everyone wait while you run to the other room to grab your notes or get some coffee. The first says, "I don't have my act together." The second says, "I don't care about your time." Again, we were a lot more careful about that stuff back when we were always meeting face to face, but virtual communication has made many of us less self-aware. And, unfortunately, there are some indications that we're bringing some of these virtual bad habits back with us into face-to-face meetings.

> **Few things are less professional than making everyone wait for you.**

If you don't already live by the mantra, "On time is late," consider adopting it for virtual meetings. Robert Love, CTO of Q-CTRL, says, "Better to be ten minutes early, than a minute late."[19] Why? Among other reasons, the added complexity of technology greatly increases the probability of something going wrong—logging in only one minute early can easily result in being ten minutes late!

Use that extra time to work through this checklist. If you're done early, spend the time reviewing your notes.

- ☐ Do I have my coffee?

- ☐ Have I used the restroom after my last five cups of coffee?

- ☐ Do I have sufficient bandwidth and is my equipment working (see Chapter 13)?

- ☐ Have I silenced my phone? (Better yet, tuck it away.)

- ☐ Do I have everything I need in easy reach, including my notes and other materials?

- ☐ Have I pulled up any files on my computer that I might need?

- ☐ Does my family/roommates know that I'm in a meeting?

- ☐ Is my dog/cat/foul-mouthed parrot (google it) locked in the next room?

- ☐ Are there any other distractions I need to put away?

---

[19] https://www.techrepublic.com/article/13-etiquette-tips-for-video-conference-calls/

❒ Will there be any garbage trucks or lawn mowers outside my window?

Better to be ten minutes early, than a minute late.

Distractions means both things that might distract the other participants (we'll cover that later) and things that distract you. Put your phone on silent (or even better, put it away), close your web browser, and clear away anything else that might pull your attention away from the meeting. Here is a good question to ask yourself, "Would I have this sitting on the table at a face-to-face meeting?

Virtual Opportunity

With a little practice, virtual meetings allow you to appear even better prepared than you actually are. If you have the relevant files easily accessible on your computer and are able to discreetly read them on screen, it will look like you have it all memorized! Warning: never use this strategy as a substitute for proper preparation. Have a good command of the primary points and keep secondary things at your fingertips.

Another unique aspect of virtual meetings is that it brings your desk to the meetings, rather than you leaving it and going to another location. This means the state of your desk becomes relevant.

"Messy desk, messy mind" and "A messy desk is a sign of genius" are two competing slogans, both of which can cite their own research.[20] But the question isn't if a messy desk is distracting—it is—but whether being distracted is a good or bad thing. Distraction paralyzes some people and breeds creativity in others. Meetings, however, are not a good place for distraction. At minimum, your messy desk should not be visible to everyone else.

---

60 Second Fix

If you're a messy desk person, experiment to see if a little organization helps you focus during meetings. Take a minute to stack some papers and move other things out of your view. Take note if that makes it easier to focus.

---

[20] https://kwiklearning.com/kwik-tips/this-is-how-a-messy-desk-affects-your-brain/ and https://medium.com/busy-building-things/why-you-should-have-a-messy-desk-c6e7b9b5bc1f, respectively.

MENTAL PREPARATION

I've said it several times already, and I'll keep repeating it. The more you put into virtual meetings, the more you'll get out of them. Don't just prepare your space, prepare your mind.

Whenever I am invited to a meeting, I want to know what it will be about. Hopefully, I'll get an actual agenda. And if the organizer forgets to fill me in, I'm not shy about asking politely. I basically say, "The more I know in advance, the more prepared and helpful I can be." There's nothing better than coming into a meeting fully prepared and at the top of your game. And there's nothing worse than that feeling of being caught unprepared.

There's nothing better than coming into a meeting at the top of your game.

Here's my suggestion. As soon as you know the meeting's purpose, estimate the amount of time you'll need to mentally prepare yourself. Double that, then schedule "prep time" at least a day in advance so you can sleep on it, but not so far in advance that you forget your thoughts.

This is important: the goal of preparation isn't to compile ammunition for your side but to ensure that you're equipped to understand and give input. Here are the sorts of things you'll want to think through:

- Is there any clarification you need in advance from the facilitator?

- Is there any information or resources you should gather?

- Wrestle through the meeting's key issues and come up with some initial (and loosely held) thoughts.

- Create several questions that will help you understand the issues and various perspectives on them.

Be sure to give yourself some time to review your notes the day of meeting. Then, just before the meeting, mentally and emotionally prepare yourself to be fully present.

Does this seem like a lot of work just to prepare for a meeting? If it makes you feel any better, I expect far more from the facilitator. But this will obviously be overkill in some situations, and sometimes you won't be given enough warning to prepare properly. But I've discovered that even ten minutes of mental preparation fifteen minutes before a meeting will enhance our ability to contribute and gain benefit. And that in turn can lead to you standing out from the crowd—for the right reasons. That's what we'll cover in the next chapter.

Being heard is the new being seen.

Chapter 5:
Show Up and Stand Out

As the COVID lockdowns hit most of the world, extroverts (like myself) found themselves going crazy before the end of the first week. Introverts (like my team member, Aimée) tried not to look too happy at the new arrangements. One novelty mug for introverts said, "I was social distancing before it was cool."

After enough time though, even introverts started feeling the isolation. Then came the Zoom explosion. While many extroverts thought it a sad substitute to grabbing a beer with a friend, many introverts found virtual meetings even more exhausting. One article on the topic was subtitled, "Experts explain why video calls are a special kind of hell for introverts."[21] The short version: web conferencing wastes a lot of emotional energy (though that energy can be recouped using my strategies).

Not surprisingly, a common response to the "virtual communication revolution" from introverts and extroverts alike has been to avoid as many meetings as they could and be minimally engaged for the ones they couldn't. There are two problems with that tactic. 1) As I said in Chapter 2, putting less energy in

---

[21] https://introvertdear.com/news/why-zoom-calls-are-draining-for-introverts/

means that your experience will be even less fulfilling and more draining. And 2) avoidance and disengagement can do serious damage to your career. There are very few people in such high demand that they can afford not to be noticed by either supervisors or potential clients—and being *heard* in meetings is the new being seen.

Being heard is the new being seen.

The goal of this chapter is to help you get the most from any virtual meeting you attend—not just through what you receive but also what you *contribute* and your opportunity to stand out in the best possible ways.

WHY ARE YOU THERE?

Why are you at the meeting? Seriously, take a moment to answer that. If your answer is, "Because I have to," you're probably missing out on some valuable opportunities to learn, contribute, and stand out.

I. LEARN

There is always something you can learn. Always. Maybe you're rolling your eyes right now and thinking "You haven't been to my meetings." Maybe not, but I've been to some pretty lame meetings (and I've led some pretty lame ones), but there was always something for me to learn, even if it was how *not* to lead a meeting—and that alone can be an incredibly valuable lesson. The point is, if you think you can't learn anything, you won't.

If you think you can't learn anything, you won't.

For many meetings, the most obvious thing to learn is its content. But don't think of your mind as a blank slate waiting to be filled. It is a field that must be prepared in order to get the maximum yield. As I said in the last chapter, study the agenda and accompanying material and complete any pre-meeting assignments. That is the minimum. From there, personally study the topic and make note of any questions. Arrive eager and ready to learn.

In the meeting itself, apply all the lessons from Chapter 2 and keep yourself completely engaged. No cell phone, no emails, no multitasking. (Remember, multitasking leads to being a half-assking.)

Aside from the content of a meeting, there are *always* plenty of lessons for the observant. Pay attention and ask yourself questions like:

- How did other participants dress? What was their set up like? How did that affect my perception of them?

- How did they interact? Did they talk too much or too little? What can I learn from that?

- What did the presenter do well? What could be improved?

There are always plenty of lessons
for the observant.

2. CONTRIBUTE

With exception of meetings that are purely presenter-focused, your participation is a key part of the meeting. Contributing and interacting engages your social mode which, in turn, creates a more positive and enjoyable experience.

This means, first of all, that your camera needs to be on and you should be utilizing all the *nonverbal* tricks in your bag:

- Waving and smiling big will communicate warmth and acceptance (even the most experienced presenter will appreciate it).

- Nodding and shaking your head shows that you're tracking with them.

- Quizzical looks can help a presenter know if they were unclear.

- And never forget to make eye contact, I mean camera contact.

When it comes to *verbal* communication, good facilitators will let you know if they prefer you to use the chat box or speak up. But if they don't, the chat box is always safest, especially in a large group.

Some participants may experience "stage fright" at the thought of speaking up. In Chapter 10, I'll touch on a few basics of public speaking as it relates to facilitators. But my suggestion for participants is to remember that this is a conversation, not a speech. There really is nothing to be afraid of.

Did that help? If not, here's a tip from my book *Speak With No Fear*: "Focus on the fun, not the fear."[22]

What I mean is, fear and joy are mutually exclusive emotions. If you focus on how your question or comment will benefit others, your fear will lessen.

You have something to add. Don't forget that. You have specific skills, experiences, and perspectives that will benefit the group. If you've done your homework and stayed engaged in the meeting, then you have something that will benefit the group. Bonus: Giving good input will help you engage and enjoy the meeting even more.

Giving good input will help you engage and enjoy the meeting even more.

Of course, some of you don't need any encouragement to contribute. In fact, you may have the opposite problem. Don't forget that the only thing worse than being a wallflower is being a blowhard. There is a skill to balancing careful listening, asking insightful questions, and offering invaluable input.

---

[22] Speak With No Fear, 2nd ed. p. 117

Not sure if you talk too much? Then there's a good chance that you do. I'm not judging—I'm in the same boat. Here's a little trick. Prior to the meeting, write down all the participants' names (yourself included) on a notepad, then use hash marks to discreetly keep track of how often everyone talks. It's the virtual meeting's equivalent of counting calories. Just by keeping track, you'll be more mindful of how much you talk. Another tip: become comfortable with silence—it isn't *always* your job to fill it! Good facilitators use silence as a "trick" to engage reluctant speakers, so you could be sabotaging them.

The only thing worse than being a wallflower is being a blowhard.

3. STAND OUT

Remember, being heard is the new being seen. With telecommuting and offsite work becoming more common, you lose opportunities to be seen around the office by the people who can help advance your career. Or if you're an entrepreneur, you may be missing a lot of prospective clients that would normally be met via informal networking. Either way, you cannot afford to miss the new opportunities that Zooming offers.

Standing out in a virtual meeting is a critical way to be remembered and help your "stock" go up in everyone's eyes. I've led hundreds of meetings and it's always the people who speak up that I remember (sometimes for the wrong reasons, but we'll get to that in a moment).

It's always the people who speak up that get remembered.

Here are seven principles that will ensure you stand out for the right reasons:

Treat every meeting like a mixture of a first date and job interview. Use everything you learn in this book. Show up on time and ready to go. Dress to impress and prepare to present your thoughts.

Be proactive, not reactive. A common complaint of hiring managers is that their team members are not proactive. They wait for instructions instead of taking initiative. That means you can "easily" stand out by being the exception. But being proactive requires bandwidth and bandwidth comes from being well prepared—you can't see the opportunities if all your attention is focused on skimming the agenda that you opened at the last minute.

Be personal and personable. Virtual communication, by virtue of being done in front of a computer, is inherently de-personalizing so you must intentionally be extra personal. This is one of the ways you "speak through the door." Allow your personality to shine through the computer screen. Don't be unattainably professional, but appropriately vulnerable and allow imperfections to slip through.

Allow your personality to shine through the computer screen.

Being personal also means having a genuine interest in the other participants. Ask questions. Remember important details. Show empathy. Be encouraging. I could rephrase this principle (and many others in this book) by saying "Have a high emotional intelligence," which is the focus of my book *Connect through Emotional Intelligence*. Emotional intelligence is arguably the most important trait for today's professional, but it's also an area where *anyone* can grow.

Remember that you are on stage. Treat every moment of the meeting as if you are being watched by everyone—because you are. Turning off your camera doesn't change that; it just means you've turned your *back* on the "audience." This doesn't have to be intimidating, though. Everyone else is on stage, too! But it means that you view everything through the lens of "How will this be perceived by others?"

I've already talked about how you dress and I'll discuss the importance of your set up (camera, lighting, backdrop, etc.) in Chapter 12. In addition, make sure to filter your *actions* through how they will be seen by the "audience." It's like this: I had a friend who worked at McDonald's in high school. They had a dedicated handwashing sink in the back room that they were required to use after going to the bathroom. This meant that for the sake of perception, he'd have to wash his hands twice, first in the bathroom and again in the backroom.

Add some pizzazz. Professional does not mean *predictable*. What makes you special? What makes you stand out in a crowd? For me, I always wear the crazy socks my son buys me—Big Foot socks, superhero socks, pizza socks…you get the idea—

even in a suit and even when the audience can't see them. I know they're there and that makes all the difference. Do you tell dad jokes? People may groan, but they'll remember it. Do you have an accent? Don't hide it. Or is there something unique in your story worth mentioning? I love the reaction I get when I say that my mom and dad were drug dealers who got straightened out and started a nonprofit mission in Mexico. Wait, what? True story. Or if you have a unique skill or hobby, don't shy away from it. I know a counselor who had won a national award for dog breeding. There is something unique about you. Don't hide it.

There is something unique about you. Don't hide it.

Choose quality over quantity. Which do you think will make you stand out more: fifty lackluster comments or one insightful observation that is so good that the presenter asks if she can use it in the future? Never talk just to be heard. Speak to make a point. Speaking of which…

Always have one big point. What makes for a memorable observation that gets noticed? It's the ability to focus a lot of talking into a single idea. One great strategy is to be the last one to speak. If you listen intently to the others, you can synthesize multiple ideas into one clear and memorable point.

VIRTUAL ETIQUETTE

Of course, you never want to be remembered for the wrong reasons—like the lady who didn't mute her mic before giving a candid (and colorful) appraisal of her company's VP. She is no longer with the company.

I cover several of these elements of virtual meeting etiquette elsewhere in this book, but it's helpful to have them collected in one spot:

- Do test your system in advance and know how everything works (we'll cover this in Chapter 13).

- Don't be the person everyone else has to wait for.

- Do shut down all unneeded files and applications.

- Don't share your screen without double-checking the above—you might accidentally share the wrong screen.

- Do make sure your pets are properly stowed and everyone in the house knows you're in a meeting.

- Don't use kid-worthy filters or backdrops (better yet, create a professional space and skip the virtual backdrop, see Chapter 13).

- Do assume that the mic and camera are on (many a memorable moment has been captured by a camera or mic that were "off.")

- Don't move your camera around and especially don't take a stroll during the meeting.

- Do silence your phone or (better) leave it in the other room.

- Don't check your phone when others are speaking.

- Do treat others with the same respect you'd want— "please" and "thank you" are still appropriate!

- Don't start or perpetuate rabbit trails.

- Do be succinct.

- Don't roll your eyes or swear.

- Do "sign off" verbally at the end of a question or comment ("That's all, thanks" or, "Anyone else?")

- Don't interrupt others—use the chat box instead (see below).

DON'T INTERRUPT, INTERJECT

Some discussions, by nature, involve a lot of back and forth. For instance, having a strict "no interruption" rule in a brainstorming meeting could stifle creativity. In those situations, my rule is "Don't interrupt, interject." Here's what I mean. I played soccer in high school, and there's a massive difference between passing the ball to a teammate who can get it closer to the goal and stealing it from your opponent.

Interrupting is the same as stealing the ball. The other person was taking the discussion one place and now you're taking it somewhere else. You've demonstrated that your goal is different from theirs and effectively made them your opponent. Interjecting is more like calling for a pass. You and the other person are working together for the same objective, and you think you have a different approach that can help everyone get closer to the goal.

Said another way, interrupting changes the subject and says, "I'm taking over" and interjecting says, "I'm with you" and builds on it. So, if you have a great, *new* idea in a discussion, write it down for later. But if you can add to what is being said, and if the meeting format permits it, then interject respectfully.

> ## Interrupting changes the subject and says, "I'm taking over" and interjecting says, "I'm with you" and builds on it.

By the way, this is great advice for communication in relationships.

TAKE RISKS

We are social creatures and fear ridicule and exclusion almost more than physical harm. That's not entirely bad. It helps us work together and "play nice." But it also keeps us from speaking up, even when we have something to say. This effect is even more pronounced when your supervisor is present. A Harvard Business Review author shared about overhearing one employee say to another, "If I tell the director what customers are saying, my career will be shot."[23] Excuse me? That's exactly the type of information management needs. But typical human behavior is driven by self-preservation: "When in doubt, keep your mouth shut." But, to stand out, you should take calculated risks.

To stand out, you must take risks.

No one has ever stood out by playing it safe. If you want to get noticed, if you want to change the conversation, if you want to get your ideas out there, you must take risks. And taking risks requires being okay with failure. If you're a driven, entrepreneurial person, then you're already comfortable with failure and risk—now just apply that to virtual meetings. Be okay with occasionally speaking out of turn or putting your foot in your mouth. So long as you keep learning from your mistakes, you're doing fine. As John Maxwell says, "Sometimes you win, sometimes you learn."

Have the courage to take risks, speak out, and stand out.

———————

Speaking of courage, leading anything takes courage. The goal of the last section was to help you *get* the most from the virtual meetings you attend. The goal of the next one is to help you *give* the most to the meetings you lead. To do that, you'll have to be willing to step in and do what others are not willing or able to do. The difference between a mediocre meeting and a great one is leadership. Are you ready to step up and lead?

---

[23] https://hbr.org/2007/05/why-employees-are-afraid-to-speak

PART THREE: **LEADING**

You have eight seconds to grab your audience's attention.

Chapter 6:
Prepare to Succeed

I recently attended a web conference call, and it began like this:

"Alright, so. Um, alright. Let's see, got this on. Um. Alright, so...I see some people are coming in... Oh, shoot. My PowerPoint. Um, let's see. If I do this..."

Painful. And a waste of everyone's time. The only reason I stayed on was because I'd been asked to evaluate the meeting.

Most Zoom presenters and facilitators don't seem to realize that turning on the camera is like stepping up to the lectern for a speech. Like it or not, that is the introduction of your presentation. Just as with any speech, the clock starts ticking immediately:

- You have eight seconds to grab your audience's attention.

- You have thirty seconds to make your first impression.

- You have two minutes to create interest.

If you haven't given them a reason to entrust you with their attention in the first five minutes, they'll start checking their email and attempting to get "real work" done.

You have eight seconds
to grab your audience's attention.

PREPARATION MAKES PERFECT

I love preparation. I may not always do it, but I always feel better when I do. Preparation increases the margins in my life and decreases the stress. By preparing everything that I can prepare for, I free up mental space for the task at hand—and for the things that can inevitably go wrong.

Preparation increases your margins and decreases your stress.

When it comes to being a presenter or facilitating a meeting, preparation is the number one difference maker, and it starts before you send out the invites. That's always been true, but virtual communication makes it easier for attendees to check out, so it's even more critical to keep them tuned in. You can complain all you want and say, "They're being paid to attend—I shouldn't have to entertain them!" But it won't change a thing. You are responsible to keep people engaged and following these steps will help you do just that.

Virtual communication makes it easier for attendees to check out, so it's even more critical to keep them tuned in.

1. DEFINE A CLEAR PURPOSE.

The single most important question you need to answer is, "Why are we meeting?" What is your purpose for taking a chunk out of everyone's time? What are the metrics for success? I know this sounds obvious, but so many facilitators don't *get* what they want because they don't *know* what they want.

Facilitators don't get what they want because they don't know what they want.

2. DETERMINE THE TYPE OF MEETING.

Your purpose will drive what kind of meeting you'll have. For instance, running an informational meeting as if it was a brainstorming meeting will fail to convey the necessary information in an authoritative way. Get this right, and your meetings will be on point and get results. Get it wrong, and they'll be a blackhole of time. These are seven basic types of meetings that I've identified:

- Informational

- Motivational

- Persuasive

- Collaborative

- Executive

- Debriefing and Feedback

- Networking and Connections

In the next chapter, I'll describe each of these and their unique challenges—and opportunities—when held virtually.

3. DECIDE WHO NEEDS TO ATTEND.

Depending on the type of meeting, you may want to limit it to those who can contribute meaningfully or expand it as far as possible. Speaking broadly, the more your meeting seeks to accomplish a task or create ideas, the more carefully you should choose your participants. Jeff Bezos, founder of Amazon, was known for his "Two Pizza Rule"—teams should be small enough to be fed by two pizzas. Why? Fewer people means quicker decisions and less groupthink.

> ### Fewer people means quicker decisions and less groupthink.

However, if your meeting's purpose is to motivate or inform, you can cast the net much further. But don't just invite people unless there is a solid reason for them to be there. Will they view this meeting as something that furthers their goals or hinders them?

I recently interviewed Carter Malloy, CEO of AcreTrader and he said he applauds employees who "fire" themselves from meetings that are irrelevant to their roles and responsibilities. If they don't know *why* they need to be there, then they don't have to be. How much time and money would that approach save your company?

4. CREATE THE AGENDA.

As we'll see later, an agenda is arguably a facilitator's most important tool. The agenda will allow you to keep your meeting focused and everyone on task. It must be driven by your purpose in #1 and shaped by the type of meeting you're facilitating.

> ## An agenda is arguably a facilitator's most important tool.

At the same time, don't make the agenda any more complicated than necessary. A "meet and greet" agenda might be:

Purpose: Introduce new members to the team.

4:00 pm: Welcome everyone and brag on new and existing members.

4:10 pm: Have everyone introduce themselves, then facilitate purposeful small talk.

4:30 pm: Close

It doesn't even have to be that detailed. The times, for instance, are just a tool to keep everyone on track—especially if you enjoy talking like I do. But an agenda can be as simple as a bulleted list of topics to cover.

Why create the agenda before sending the invitations? To make sure you actually complete it, first of all. Furthermore, creating the agenda will help you refine your purpose, evaluate your invitation list, and better estimate the meeting's length. Most importantly, a written agenda eliminates the most dreaded type of meeting: the "meet just to meet" meeting. By the way, if writing the agenda results in you canceling the meeting, that will be a win in everyone's book!

5. SET THE TIME AND DATE.

Don't schedule the meeting until you know who needs to be there. Why? Because that will guide how hard you'll work to accommodate competing schedules. Better to have that one person whose insight is always invaluable than those five people who will scroll on their phones the whole time.

Be strategic about the date and time. Studies have shown that, for most people, Mondays and Tuesdays are the most productive days of the week. Not surprisingly, productivity declines as the week draws to a close. Likewise, people tend to be more focused in the mornings than the afternoons.

Here's how to use that information for setting the time and date. Imagine that you'll have to pay each of the participants based upon when the meeting is held. Monday and Tuesday mornings are the most expensive. Lunches and Friday afternoons are cheapest. Does your meeting require paying for the premium time? Some meetings do, especially meetings that set the agenda for the week or require a high level of focus. Other meetings, such as "meet and greets" do not.

By the way, this isn't just an act of imagination. Time isn't money; time x efficiency is. A low priority meeting during someone's highest efficiency time effectively steals money from them or the company.

> **A low priority meeting during someone's highest efficiency time effectively steals money from them or the company.**

6. SCHEDULE THE MEETING.

It's finally time to pull the trigger. When you send the invites, I'd encourage you not only to attach the agenda, but include a "purpose statement" in the body of the email. By being as clear and specific as possible, you set everyone up for success. Don't just give the when and *what*, but also the *why* and *how to prepare*. Examples:

> "Our new project management software will be a game changer...but there will be a bit of a learning curve. On Thursday, we'll have a mandatory training session to get us all on the same page."

> "It's your favorite time of year—budget meeting! Please send me your proposal by next Tuesday so I can distribute them ahead of time."

"This Friday, we're hosting a virtual happy hour to welcome our new hires. Grab your favorite beverage and let them know what it's really like to work at Acme!"

Don't just give the when and what, but also the why and how to prepare.

Depending on the type of meeting, you may want to include specific questions that you'll be asking. And think through "supplementary materials" you can send, maybe a helpful blog about brainstorming or a bio on the guest presenter. Be clear whether the material is suggested or required reading (and be ready to hold them accountable to it).

The invitation should give clear instructions on what platform you'll be using, what they need to bring, and how to join the meeting. Either send a link or let them know when you'll do so. And, obviously, make sure that the meeting is private and/or password protected to keep lurkers away.

One more thing: Be clear that you'll start promptly and encourage them to arrive a couple minutes early in case there are any "technical difficulties." Technical difficulties are the traffic jams of virtual communication—always give yourself extra time to account for them.

Technical difficulties are the traffic jams of virtual communication—always give yourself extra time to account for them.

WHAT DO YOU EXPECT?

Does it feel like you should be ready to meet now?

Not quite.

Once you've defined your purpose, determined the type of meeting, decided who needs to attend, created the agenda, set the time and date, and scheduled the meeting, *now* is the time to write out your expectations for the meeting.

Why? Because participants can't meet expectations that you don't communicate. Sounds obvious, but I've watched it happen again and again. Facilitators fail to set and communicate expectations then get frustrated at the participants! For example, maybe I expected the participants of my informational meeting to interact with me via the chat, but they didn't because I didn't set that expectation.

Unexpressed expectations turn into unmet expectations which turn into frustrations.

60 Second Fix

Do you want your team or the attendees to interact using the chat feature? Set the expectation early on and start by asking for some simple interaction. For example, at the beginning of the meeting, you can say, "I really want everyone to participate via the chat, so let's all practice right now. Type in where you were born." Then you should comment on their responses. Does this feel familiar? I'm sure you've seen plenty of professional webinars use this trick.

Here is the key point: you can't set the expectations if you don't know what they are. You already know your purpose for the meeting, but what do you want from the participants in order to achieve that purpose? Here are some possible examples:

- Study the agenda in advance.

- Come to the meeting with five ideas or questions.

- Leave their camera on and mic off (or on!).

- Not look at their phone.

- Interrupt with clarifying questions

- Not interrupt with questions but wait for Q & A.

- Give feedback in the chat.

- Take notes.

- Use nonverbal communication (nodding, thumbs up, etc.)

- Respond to your questions.

Did you notice how many of the above expectations are contradictory? You simply can't expect everyone to intuitively know what you want. In the face of that uncertainty, most people will choose the safest option of doing nothing. Expressing your expectations provides certainty to the participants.

Share your expectations prior to, and at the beginning of, the meeting. You can then turn those *expressed* expectations into *actionable* expectations. Then, over time, consistently applied expectations create culture. As the meeting progresses, keep reminding the participants of them. They need to know, for instance, that you actually want them to ask questions.

Consistently applied expectations create culture.

The funny thing is that you probably already understand this principle, but we don't always carry it over into virtual meetings.

As I said, a lot of this information applies to face-to-face meetings just as much as virtual ones. If you apply these principles, your meetings will get better. That's also true of the next chapter, but I'm also going to show you ways that virtual communication can actually make your meetings *better* than in-person.

There are few things as enjoyable and productive
as a well-led gathering of great minds.

Chapter 7

Know Your Meetings

Years ago, I was hired as the president of a non-profit organization that had millions of dollars in debt, a dwindling customer base, and a host of other problems. The board meetings were routinely five plus hours long and not very effective. The first hour—or maybe two—were spent "connecting," followed by some sort of training or discussion. By the time we got down to making truly critical decisions, everyone's attention span was already waning and participants became increasingly distracted. The lack of emotional energy allowed the board to be easily sidetracked by little fires that could have been handled by the staff.

Here's the problem. They were trying to hold three meetings in one—relational, informational, and executive—and not doing any of them well. I fixed it by enforcing a hard three-hour limit. After that, I'd literally stand up and say, "Thanks for coming. See you next month!" Suddenly, everyone got serious about our primary purpose: making the high-level decisions only the board could make.

Knowing what kind of meeting you're leading and structuring it accordingly will make all the difference between success and failure. Do this right and people will want to come to your meeting because they know they'll get something out of it.

> ## Knowing what kind of meeting you're leading will make all the difference between success and failure.

PRELIMINARY QUESTIONS

Different experts will categorize the different types of meetings differently and the lines between them will blur, so my seven are not the final word.[24] They are meant to provide you with a good framework to be tailored to your specific needs. Begin by asking the following two basic questions:

1. Is the purpose of this meeting to a) share information or b) initiate action?

2. Should this meeting be a) participant-focused (interactive and soliciting input) or b) presenter-focused (non-interactive)?

I'll clarify these in a minute, but don't make the mistake of thinking there is a "right" answer—there's a time and place for each type. For instance, people seem to think that "interactive is always best," but when I'm listening to a TED talk, the last thing I want is for Brené Brown to be interrupted by someone sharing about their pet bunny.

---

[24] Two great resources are https://www.pgi.com/blog/2020/04/9-types-of-business-meetings/ and https://blog.lucidmeetings.com/blog/16-types-of-business-meetings.

I'm sure you also noticed that these aren't necessarily either/or questions. They're more like two intersecting continuums:

INITIATE ACTION

PRESENTER FOCUSED   PARTICIPANT FOCUSED

SHARE INFORMATION

With that in mind, here are the seven basic types of meetings:

1. **Informational**

2. **Motivational**

3. **Persuasive**

4. **Collaborative**

5. **Executive**

6. **Debriefing and Feedback**

7. **Networking and Connections**

And here is where they *roughly* sit on the graph:

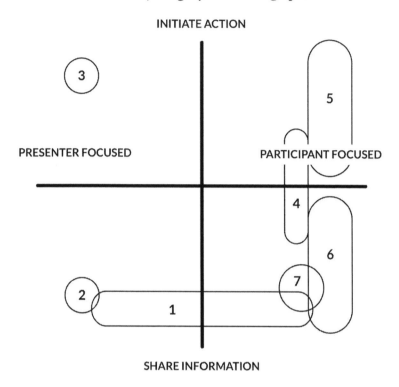

On the left are the presenter-focused meetings. That doesn't mean the meeting is about the presenter. In fact, (soapbox warning!) meetings are always about the participants, never the presenter. That's one of the seven principles in my book, *Speak With No Fear.* Your job is always to serve the listener/participants. The question is if the *content* comes from the presenter or the participants. Said another way, will you be more of a *presenter* of content or *facilitator* of discussions?

So, both **motivational** and **persuasive** meetings are *presenter-focused,* driven by the material that you (as the presenter) bring.

But **persuasive** meetings attempt to influence action—getting the participants to buy or buy into something. **Motivational** meetings, on the other hand, are trying to make the participants think or feel something.

Informational meetings, as we'll see, can *either* be presenter-focused (a TED Talk), participant-focused (a roundtable discussion), or somewhere between (like an interactive workshop).

The rest of the meetings are decidedly *participant-focused*. Your job in these ones is to facilitate the discussion, i.e., to help *them* share *their* content. By the way, that doesn't mean these meetings are easier—I put more work into participant-focused meetings.

Collaborative meetings (such as brainstorming) focus more on creating and sharing ideas, while **executive** (defined here in the sense of "carrying out a plan" as opposed to "persons having authority") meetings focus on making decisions and creating an action plan. **Debriefing and feedback** is unique in that it begins by assessing (information) and ends with making decisions about next time (action). Finally, **Networking and connections** is the furthest from action—nothing gets *done* at these meetings (but they are crucial for future action).

---

60 Second Fix

One simple way to communicate whether your meeting will be presenter-focused or participant-focused is intentionally using speaker view for the former and gallery view for the latter. Actually, it's more of a one second fix (click a button), but it will set the tone profoundly. Before you start your meeting, decide which one you'll use and why.

Now let's focus on each type of meeting and especially how virtual communication affects them.

I. INFORMATIONAL

The purpose of this meeting is to inform, train, or teach, but can be either presenter-focused or participant-focused (or somewhere in between). Start by deciding which one yours will be. Another way of saying this is that participation can come in the form of *input* or *interaction*. It's important to understand the difference:

Input means that the attenders are adding to the content. This is a double-edged sword. The participants may have some great perspective and be able to add significantly to an informational meeting. But those with the least to say are frequently the most inclined to talk. If you're going to solicit input—asking, "Does anyone have any thoughts?", for instance—be sure you have a plan for keeping it under control, and the courage to do so. We've all experienced meetings hijacked by someone who liked to hear themselves talk. Keeping control is even more important in virtual meetings because it's easier for the rest of the participants to check out during the rant, never to return.

Interaction means creating questions and exercises to help the participants internalize and contextualize your content. If you think back to some of your favorite instructors, they probably made good use of interaction. This is what I do in most of my workshops, such as "10 Speaking Skills in 60 Minutes." I interact with the participants to create a more enjoyable learning opportunity and help them apply the material, but I'm not looking for input. I won't allow one participant to hijack the meeting with his theories of communication. And the rest of participants really appreciate me keeping the meeting under control and productive.

Keep meetings under control so that they're productive and enjoyable for the majority.

As you plan the informational meeting, decide how much input and interaction you want. Here are three rules of thumb:

Use interaction for complicated information or ideas that need to be contextualized for individual situations. Prepare discussion questions and interactive exercises. Not only do these help the participants learn, but they're the best way to gauge their actual comprehension. Why? Because most people will say they understand, even if they really don't. Asking questions reveals the truth.

Solicit input if the participants are knowledgeable on the topic. I've facilitated meetings where the attendees knew more than me and I learned more than they did. There's nothing wrong with that—unless you're too proud or foolish to ask and listen!

If the topic is straightforward, limit interaction to set Q&A times. In these situations, I'll say, "Today, I'm going to talk to you about X. At the end, we'll have an optional Q&A time, so type your questions in the chat as we go." (Note: I set my expectations at the beginning.) The people who quickly understand the information *love* me for saving them from the torture of obvious questions.

Another important point: these meetings have no minimum length, but they should have a maximum. If everyone "gets it", end the meeting—I promise, no one will complain!

If everyone "gets it", end the meeting—I promise, no one will complain!

VIRTUAL CHALLENGES AND OPPORTUNITIES

The challenge of virtual informational meetings is that participation—especially asking questions—is not as natural or free flowing. You'll need to be even more intentional by setting the expectations ("Use the chat box," "Chime in!", etc.) and keeping them accountable. My favorite tool is the *awkward pause*.

Use their discomfort with silence "against" them by letting them know that you'll wait as long as it takes.

The first virtual advantage is how much more professional and effective your material can be with the use of presentation software. Second, you can easily record your presentation and make it available to a wider audience later.

Important note: I'm not a lawyer and can't offer any legal advice, but it's important to know that laws regarding recording meetings vary from state to state, as do laws about using those recordings later. You are responsible to know and abide by these laws.

Legalities aside, it's simply good manners to clearly inform participants that you'll be recording it (which Zoom now does automatically) and also let them know that you'll be using the recording in the future. And be sure to get permission from the organization as well.

2. MOTIVATIONAL:

The goal, obviously, is to motivate and inspire the attendees to think and feel differently. Think of these as the pep rallies of meetings. You're trying to get people excited about something and rallying them to some objective. This might be a personal objective (become more confident) or business (sell the new product).

As I said, motivational meetings are presenter-focused. They don't have a lot of genuine interaction. But don't pep rallies have lots of shouting and cheers? Yes, but that's different from soliciting input. If Tony Robbins shouts to a filled auditorium "What will it take for you to make your next step?", he's looking for cheers, not suggestions.

VIRTUAL CHALLENGES AND OPPORTUNITIES

The challenge of virtual motivational meetings is that it's harder to push your energy over the distance. Harder, but not impossible. You must be very intentional about speaking through the door (see Chapter 2).

The virtual advantage is that it's much easier, and cheaper, to engage a larger number of people. If you had a large enough platform, you could literally give a motivational talk this afternoon on Facebook to millions, for free.

Additionally, you can use presentation tools to make an incredibly engaging meeting. Inspirational background music? Video testimonials? No problem.

3. PERSUASIVE:

Persuasive meetings are like motivational meetings but with the significant difference that you want the participants to do something specific. A sales presentation is a persuasive meeting—you want your audience to buy your coaching package, for instance. So is pitching your ideas to the CEO. So is creating buy-in from your team. So is a job interview. In all these cases, your goal is getting the audience engaged in specific actions.

A sales presentation is a persuasive meeting.

Like the motivational meeting, this is presenter-focused. You aren't soliciting the participants' input except to further your purpose of persuading them. That doesn't mean you aren't listening very carefully to their responses. They provide invaluable feedback for improving your presentation—or even your "product."

VIRTUAL CHALLENGES AND OPPORTUNITIES

Virtual persuasive meetings are unique in that we've been doing them for a long time—a sales call is a virtual persuasive meeting. Their challenge lies in fully engaging the participants and using more energy than you would in person. If you aren't a natural salesperson, you'll need to practice this to get over your self-consciousness.

In addition to the ability to reach more people more easily, the virtual advantage here is that technology allows for a seamless Call To Action (CTA). You can ask your participants to click a button, sign up for your email list, or schedule an appointment without leaving your page.

4. COLLABORATIVE:

A collaborative meeting is all about utilizing a variety of perspectives, expertise, and opinions to gain better ideas. There are few meetings as enjoyable and productive as a well-led gathering of great minds. As they say, "No one of us is as smart as all of us."

There are few things as enjoyable and productive as a well-led gathering of great minds.

Brainstorming sessions are the most familiar form of collaborative meetings. These, by nature, are very open ended and foster the greatest creativity when practicality is completely ignored and there is plenty of time for crazy ideas. **Problem solving** meetings are also collaborative, but are more focused and very much interested in practical limitations. **Conflict resolution** is also a type of collaborative meeting.

There is a lot of great information about leading these meetings, but it's important to know that they require more, not less, preparation and active guidance. There's an art to negotiating conflicting opinions, encouraging less vocal participants to speak up, and allowing discussion to flow organically without getting off-track. A well-written agenda, sent out in advance, will prime the pump and set the stage for a great discussion.

VIRTUAL CHALLENGES AND OPPORTUNITIES

The challenge of virtual collaborative meetings is the diminished back-and-forth, talking-over-each-other interaction. But, with practice, participants can gain a new rhythm. Also be sure to encourage the use of the chat feature to keep ideas popping even when others are talking.

The virtual advantage comes from software—like Microsoft Teams—that allow participants to easily share files, doodle on virtual whiteboards, and access information quickly.

5. EXECUTIVE:

As I said earlier, I'm using "executive" in the adjectival sense of "relating to carrying out plans or duties" as opposed to the noun "persons having authority." Like collaborative meetings, executive meetings are very much participant-driven, but they are ultimately about making decisions and getting things done.

Side note: Can you see how important clarifying the type of meeting is? If you think you're at an executive meeting when it's actually collaborative, you'll be extremely frustrated by all the "pointless talking." Other way around, and you'll feel rushed and invalidated.

Any project or enterprise involving multiple people will require keeping them on the same page (which makes executive meetings great for "silo busting"). Some information will need to be shared, such as updates from each team member, then the focus can be shifted to fixing the problems and planning next steps.

If it's well executed (pun intended), a good executive meeting can be exhilarating—a real or virtual room full of driven, dedicated, and bright people can accomplish more in fifteen minutes than most people can in a week. But, because they're frequently ongoing (e.g. a weekly "direct reports" meeting), they are also the most prone to "meeting for the sake of meeting." As the facilitator, your job is to encourage efficiency. Have an agenda, set time limits, and reward your team with praise for running short.

Reward what you want repeated.

VIRTUAL CHALLENGES AND OPPORTUNITIES

The challenges of virtual executive meetings are finding a good rhythm of talking and listening and the difficulty of reading nonverbal communication. Because these meetings can be more "down to business," it's important for everyone to keep their camera turned on and to be very mindful of how they are being perceived. These meetings require both well-established rules to maintain the rhythm of discussion and decisions and also an engaged facilitator that keeps things on track while ensuring that the insightful but soft-spoken voices are heard. Consider using speaker view when each participant is giving their update then switching to gallery for the discussion. And encourage full use of the chat box.

The virtual advantage is that it's much easier to get all the key players involved, even if they're halfway across the world. They are also built for efficiency—if someone had to drive thirty minutes to attend a meeting, they'd feel obligated to meet for at least that long. Virtual meetings can skip the small talk, sprint through agenda, and log off in five minutes if that's all that is needed.

6. DEBRIEFING:

I'm a big believer in debriefing meetings. "Those who forget the past are doomed to repeat it" applies here. Whenever I give a big speech or put on some event, I always take time to celebrate what worked and examine what didn't. This is best done as a separate meeting with a handful of insightful individuals, but even a solo debriefing is better than none.

Those who forget the past are doomed to repeat it.

As I said, these meetings are unique in that they are about both information (the observations gathered) and action (what to do differently next time).

VIRTUAL CHALLENGES AND OPPORTUNITIES

The challenge of virtual debriefing meetings is getting people to fully engage. As with the collaborative meetings, it's easy for one or two people to do most of the talking and the rest to disengage. Communicate your expectations and strategically engage the quieter participants (saying, "I'd love to hear from someone who hasn't yet shared," for instance). Also set your expectations before the event—let them know about the debrief meeting (I like to plan mine the day after) and ask them to be ready to discuss two things that worked and two that didn't.

The virtual advantage is that you are easily able to record your findings in real time, using project managing software or even just a Word document. And you can also record the meeting itself so that, a year later, you aren't trying to remember what the note "More cowbell" meant. Additionally, it's much easier to coordinate virtual debriefing meetings.

7. NETWORKING AND CONNECTIONS:

Whether you're an extrovert or an introvert, you know how important networking and personal connections are in the business world. That's why people joke, "Alcohol—it's how work gets done." It's not the beer; it's the relationships built. With the COVID lockdowns, meet and greets had to go virtual and many have struggled to adapt, but connection isn't any less important. In addition to networking, this category also includes team building meetings or any other meeting where the primary purpose is getting to know each other (if you are interested in doing more celebratory team connection meetings, consider checking out Kahoot which easily integrates into Zoom).

VIRTUAL CHALLENGES AND OPPORTUNITIES

The challenge of virtual networking meetings is that they feel less personal. This is where switching from solo to social mode becomes crucial. I'm not saying a virtual happy hour is as much fun as a real one, but that's no excuse to not make the extra effort to engage others.

Once again, a capable facilitator is vital. You have to have a good list of questions that allow participants to share person-alities, abilities, and experiences without feeling like they're bragging. Here are some suggestions:

- What do others find most interesting about you?

- Describe a great day at the office—one that leaves you "good tired."

- Would you rather your work to be good and on-time or perfect and late?

- What resources or expertise are you most in need of right now?

The virtual advantage is that you're able to focus on talking. Too often, connection meetings become about something other than connecting. In a previous executive role, I once took my staff indoor skydiving as a team building activity, but skydiving became the only focus. Was it fun? Sure, and I have the pictures to prove it, but it didn't accomplish my purpose.

Hopefully, it's becoming clear that with proper preparation, virtual meetings can be incredibly effective. You should also notice that being a top-notch facilitator will increase your personal success and enhance your value to your organization. But all that work will be wasted if you choke in the meeting itself. Over the next couple chapters, I'll give you some incredibly practical advice on how to kill it (in a good way) after you log on.

Pointless meetings are a failure of leadership.

Chapter 8:
Start Strong

Have you ever used words like these to describe a virtual meeting: Boring, pointless, awkward, frustrating, a train wreck, complete waste of time, hell-on-earth? Take a moment to examine what made you feel that way (everything is a learning opportunity, right?). Maybe it was that...

- A participant was allowed to dominate the conversation.

- Conversely, no one wanted to talk.

- The meeting just meandered purposelessly for an hour.

- The meeting accomplished its purpose, *then* meandered purposelessly for an hour.

- A presenter had little to say but spent ninety minutes saying it.

- The meeting turned into a conversation between two people.

- The meeting that turned into an *argument* between two people.

- People arrived late and fumbled with their equipment, each delay costing you input that you needed.

- There was thirty minutes of small talk before diving into the agenda.

What do all of these scenarios have in common? A failure of leadership. Great leaders (and facilitators *are* leaders) would ensure equal opportunities and a clear purpose. They would set expectations and enforce them. They would keep everyone on track, even if it was uncomfortable for them.

Pointless meetings are a failure of leadership.

This is another soapbox of mine: great leaders come to serve. As a consultant and coach, I may select my engagements and coaching opportunities based upon *my* goals, but once I show up, my entire focus shifts to *their* goals. I shove myself out of the way and serve them. Put another way, it's not about me.

That is the attitude I want you to have: Facilitating a meeting is not about you, it's about the participants. I don't care if it's a motivational, informational, persuasive, collaborative, or executive meeting—if you aren't there to serve them, you're using and manipulating them. And they will know it.

Facilitating a meeting is not about you, it's about the participants.

The good news is that "it's not about me" can make leading less intimidating. For example, it's easier to call out a rabbit trail if you know that everyone is secretly thrilled that you did so.

Let's dive into what strong leadership means for meetings.

PRE-MEETING

Whenever I speak at an in-person event, I always arrive early enough to get ready, make sure everything is in place, and still have time to mingle with the participants. This is one of my seven strategies for speaking without fear. By getting to know some of them, I feel like I know all of them, and it's a lot less scary to talk to friends than strangers. I do this even if I already know the audience. Chatting with them helps me read the room. If, for instance, I find out that a well-loved employee just got diagnosed with cancer, I'll cut my opening joke. Said another way, I arrive early so I can serve them better.

It's less scary to talk to friends than strangers.

That principle still holds with virtual meetings, but the practice is a little bit different. If I'm speaking to a group that is new to me, I use some of the many tools available to me (e.g., Facebook or LinkedIn) to get to know some of them. Then I'm always on five minutes early and chat with any early comers. To clarify—this is five minutes *on top of* whatever time I need to make sure everything is set up and ready to go. Depending on the event and my role, I might check in with the event's organizer half an hour earlier. We'll do a soundcheck, make sure all my slides and resources are working, and do a quick rehearsal. Taking care of all that early on leaves me with extra bandwidth to interact.

Now, if I'm coming to a meeting as an outside presenter, I'll leave my camera off pre-meeting and display my speaker's "headshot"—this communicates professionality and allows the emcee to introduce me—but I'll still be "mingling" via the chat box. I'll ask the participants where they're from and about their job, etc. However, if I'm functioning as a facilitator with a group I already know, I'll have my camera turned on as I "mingle." This models my expectation that all participants have their cameras on.

TO SERVE AND ENFORCE

In Chapter 5, we focused on having a clear purpose, sending the agenda in advance, and knowing your expectations. Now it's time to enforce that agenda and those expectations.

Here's the most important principle: begin on time and hit the ground running. As I said earlier, you have less than five minutes from when you go live to persuade the participants to give you their whole attention—don't waste it.

You have less than five minutes to persuade the participants to give you their whole attention.

Additionally, starting on time sets expectations for future meetings. Don't make the mistake of starting late to accommodate latecomers. Some people are perpetually late, so if they know that you start five minutes late, they're going to come ten minutes late. However, depending on the culture of the company, you can be a little loose on how you define "on-time." One team I worked with decided to start exactly two minutes past to give a little grace period for technical difficulties (I wouldn't do any more than five, and that's pushing it). With that team, I could also text anyone that was missing during that time. But we didn't let that grace period creep up—it stayed at two minutes week after week.

Important note: There are, of course, exceptions. Just as weddings always start a little late, some one-time events are important enough to delay. And sometimes there are key players that you must wait for, especially in persuasive (sales) meetings.

Exceptions aside, start the meeting on time, boldly welcoming everyone and reminding them of the meeting's purpose. Resist the urge to use filler to buy time for the late comers. Every minute you delay for latecomers costs you the attention of punctual participants.

Every minute you delay for latecomers costs you the attention of punctual participants.

Here's a better strategy: launch the meeting on time and, when it seems like the latecomers have all arrived, greet them as a group (rather than individually which wastes time and breaks your flow) and quickly summarize any key information they'll need for the rest of the meeting. Or you can direct them to watch the video later.

So, after starting on time and stating the meeting's purpose, share your expectations (Chapter 5). It could sound like this:

> "Good afternoon, everyone! It's good to have you here. As you know, we start on time and are ready to create. I see we still have some people joining us, but I'll catch them up later.
>
> I trust you all had time to go over the agenda, but if you don't have it handy, you'll see it posted in the chat as well.
>
> The purpose of this meeting is to _____. I'd like you all to keep your cameras on, but please mute your mics when you're not talking.
>
> I'm going to start by briefly talking about _____, and then we'll begin our discussion. If you have any questions during my opening, please use the chat so I can answer them at the end. In fact, why don't we practice using the chat box right now? If you have any questions about the game plan, type them in the chat right now. If you don't, just type 'No questions' so I know everyone is familiar with the tool.
>
> I'll give you a minute… Okay, great. Still waiting for a couple of you… Jim, do you see where the chat tool is at? Great, that's all of you. Here is what you need to know (insert official opening line to your presentation here such as 'we are up 32% from last quarter')."

Notice what happened here:

"Good afternoon, everyone! It's good to have you here. We start on time and are ready to create."

A short, warm greeting, followed by one-line reinforcement of your company's culture, in this case punctuality and creativity, but you should change this to something that emphasizes your culture, especially as it relates to the meeting.

"I see we still have some people joining us late, but I'll catch them up later."

You're setting everyone at ease by acknowledging the "late-comer issue." What I mean is that, if you were clear about expecting everyone to arrive on time, people will wonder how you'll respond to those who don't. This kind of response doesn't ignore their tardiness, but communicates, "I have this completely under control." And that's what the participants want to know.

Participants want to know that you have everything under control.

"I trust you all had time to go over the agenda, but if you don't have it handy, you'll see it posted in the chat as well."

Again, you're expressing your expectation (read agenda prior to meeting), but also proactively deals with anyone who forgot theirs.

"So, the purpose of this meeting is to _____. I'd like you all to keep your cameras on, but please mute your mics when you're not talking."

Remind them of the meeting's purpose and explain more of your expectations.

"I'm going to start by briefly talking about _____, and then we'll begin our discussion. If you have any questions during my opening, please use the chat so I can answer them at the end."

Now you're letting them know what they can expect, then providing clear directions. By now, they're thinking, "This facilitator knows what they're doing! Maybe this meeting won't be a waste."

"In fact, why don't we practice using the chat box right now. If you have any questions about the game plan, type them in the chat right now. If you don't, just type 'No questions' so I know everyone is familiar with the tool."

Not only are you ensuring they know how to chat, you're getting them in the habit at the beginning.

"I'll give you a minute… Okay, great. Still waiting for a couple of you… Jim, do you see where the chat tool is at? Great, that's all of you."

This demonstrates that you mean business, but calmly and with confidence. By the way, virtual communication is not like FM radio—dead air is not your enemy. It's a tool. Nothing displays confidence like sipping coffee while patiently waiting for people to respond.

Nothing displays confidence like sipping coffee while patiently waiting for people to respond.

Here is what you need to know (insert official opening line)."

No small talk, no filler, just straight into the material.

By setting the tone early, it will be exponentially easier to keep it going as the meeting continues. But if you don't take control at the beginning, it will be exponentially more difficult to regain it.

Maybe you're thinking "Take control? I want this to be more, I don't know, democratic." Democracy and anarchy are not the same thing. We want people to lead and enforce the rules, to protect the weak from the strong. Again, you are serving the participants and respecting their time by providing direction.

The *way* you provide direction will be driven by your temperament—I've known sweet old ladies who can keep order better than a drill sergeant—but you will still have to be courageous and engage your leadership skills.

So, you need to start strong and continue strong. Work your way through the agenda by gently but firmly, keeping the meeting on task.

That's not to say never go off script. A good leader will recognize when to adjust and adapt. Sometimes a chance comment will shed light on a massive issue that needs to be addressed. But there's a difference between going off script and letting a meeting be hijacked. The difference is (you guessed it) leadership.

There's a difference between going off script and letting a meeting be hijacked.

A MULTI-BILLION DOLLAR PROBLEM

One article reported that excessive and inefficient meetings cost a combined total of $37,000,000,000.[25] That's a lot of money, which is why it's important for you to understand that unnecessary and poorly run meetings are costing your organizations real money.

I was hired by a multi-location car dealership in the Midwest that was extremely successful but recognized they needed to improve their communications—it often takes an outside view to see what you've become blind to. As I audited their meetings, I discovered a massive hole in their budget. I walked the CEO through the math:

They had 1,000 employees and they attended, on average, three one-hour team meetings a week. That might sound like a little or a lot depending on your profession, but it was reasonable for their industry and culture. However, as I sat in on several meetings, I discovered that a full *twenty minutes* of each meeting was wasted. A certain amount of small talk is vital in any relationship-driven business, so I wasn't including that. This was a straight twenty minutes completely wasted due to poorly run meetings. That works out to 1,000 hours of productivity per *week*.

Their average salary was $30 an hour (which, when you consider benefits and taxes, is lower than average because commissions weren't included), so that equated to $30,000 they were wasting

---

[25] https://www.fool.com/careers/2018/07/26/is-your-company-having-too-many-meetings.aspx

per week. That got the CEO's attention! Suddenly, my value as a consultant had a real number behind it. By teaching his team the material you are reading here and then coaching their facilitators through trimming five minutes here and ten minutes there, I put money back into everyone's pockets.

Take a minute and do the math for your company or department. How many hours a week does the average employee in your company or department spend in a meeting?

Of those hours, how many are wasted? Based on my experience, the first ten minutes of every meeting is wasted on latecomers, getting people settled in, and uninteresting introductions. At least another ten minutes are lost to inefficiency (though sometimes much more), an additional five to ten gets lost in transitions between subjects or speakers, then another five to meandering closings of the meeting.

Now ask yourself if every participant needs to be at every meeting they attend. If your employee is at a meeting they don't need to be at, then 100% of their time is being wasted. And it gets worse: if the meeting itself is unnecessary (as many meetings are), then 100% of *everyone's* time is wasted. Put all that together and estimate how many hours a week are being wasted.

If a meeting is unnecessary, then 100% of everyone's time is wasted.

Next, what is the average salary (remembering to include benefits and taxes)? Now is the most painful step. How much money are you losing to ineffective and unnecessary meetings?

Ouch.

By the way, this still applies if you're in a non-profit with an all-volunteer team. Their time is worth money and not respecting it will cost you volunteers in the long run.

Here's the equation you need to use as you go into every meeting:

$$S \times P \div 60 = \$$$

That is, the average hourly salary, times the number of participants, divided by sixty minutes equals the cost per minute of your meeting. With that number in your head, you'll learn to see each wasted minute as money going up in smoke. After that, you might start being a little less indulging of "Always-late-Linda" and "Won't-shut-up-Satya."

Learn to see each wasted minute as money going up in smoke.

The point is not, of course, to not have meetings. An effective meeting that brings all the right people together can save hours' worth of forwarded and CC'd emails. The key is keeping them effective. In my experience, facilitating great discussions is the single most important skill you can develop for that, which is our next topic.

Your job isn't to encourage discussion,
but to encourage productive discussion.

Chapter 9:
Facilitating Great Interaction

I've explained about how virtual communication requires "talking through the door"—being more deliberate in order to push through the medium's inherent limitations. It's learning to overcome the drawbacks and capitalizing on the advantages.

The most obvious limitation of Zooming is the loss of effortless back and form conversations. Gone are the countless micro connections in face-to-face meetings. I've already covered multiple strategies for participants who want to talk through that door. Now let's focus on the facilitator's role.

Even before the COVID lockdowns, I learned that virtual meetings need more *planned* interaction to make up for all the missing incidental interaction of in-person meetings. For example, I can easily do a live 45-60 minute keynote speech and people will remain engaged. They're able to interact with each other and I'm able to interact with them via personal eye contact and banter. But in a Zoom meeting, the longest I'll go without soliciting some sort of interaction is ten minutes (ideally, more like every seven minutes).

Virtual meetings need more planned interaction to make up for missing incidental interaction.

What kind of interaction?

That depends entirely on the type of meeting. If it's more presenter-focused, I'll want interaction that keeps the participants interested and ensures that they understand the content. But if it's participant-focused, I'll want interaction that empowers them to play an active role. Your three main tools are:

1. Chat boxes

2. Real time discussions

3. Breakout rooms

Each of them have specific advantages and should be used intentionally to accomplish your purpose. For the rest of this chapter, we'll look at each one and end with some miscellaneous tips for facilitating great interaction.

Important note: Everything ahead assumes you already have a good working relationship with your team. What I mean is that, if you've already created a culture of open interaction, then you'll be able to transfer that to virtual interactions. If not, then you probably need to work on your emotional intelligence first. There are many great tools for this, including my most recent book, *Connect through Emotional Intelligence* and its accompanying workbook.

CHAT BOX

Say it with me, "The chat box is your friend." Thanks to texting, almost everyone is comfortable with this streamlined form of communication. What makes it so valuable is that it allows conversations (either to the entire group or between individuals) to happen without disrupting the flow of the meeting. And it's also much more *efficient* because everyone can type at once. Asking ten people to share their hobby could take five minutes in a real time discussion (more if anyone is a rambler), but 30 seconds via chat.

The chat box is your friend.

As I demonstrated in the last chapter, the key is getting people to use the chat early on and continually reinforcing that expectation. Here are some of the things to use chat for:

- Ensuring participants are actually present and engaged.

- Responding to a question posed to the entire group.

- Making observations or asking questions about the speaker's content.

- Emoticon reactions to what's being said.

- Discreet side communication (more on that shortly).

- Links to relevant articles or resources.

One more note: Some people struggle with written communication on the fly. Maybe they're slow typists or have a specific challenge, such as dyslexia or not being a native English speaker. For that reason, never call out bad grammar or spelling. Just do your best to understand their intended meaning from context. If you can't, then privately ask for clarification—using the direct chat function! And if someone is exceptionally reluctant to engage in chats, it may be wise to inquire later on if there's a deeper issue.

DISCUSSION REFEREE

Real time discussion is your most important interaction tool—some things just can't be communicated via text—and is essential for participant-focused meetings. But it's also the most prone to getting out of hand and is the #1 source of wasted time (and hence money).

It's time to step up and lead.

Real time discussion is prone to getting out of hand and is the #1 source of wasted time and money.

As I said, I played a lot of soccer in high school and was a reasonably good forward. I remember one game that had a higher-than-average rivalry between us and the other team. For whatever reason, this one guy just seemed against me from the beginning. I mean, it was more than smack talk. He just didn't like me. So, it felt great when I stole the ball from him and scored immediately—but it didn't improve his attitude towards me at all.

Not much later, I stole the ball again and started heading down the field to take another shot. I felt him literally jump on me from behind and I tumbled to the ground. Filled with all the testosterone of a high school boy, I turned around, ready to throw a punch and both teams converged on us. I was halted by the harsh whistle of the referee. He pulled the other boy away and laid into him. I got a penalty kick, and he got a yellow card. Maybe the other kid deserved more than a warning, but I know that the ref's quick response prevented a full-on brawl between our teams. Referees are crucial to keeping players focused and moving the game forward.

Discussions are a crucial element of most meetings, especially those that are participant-focused. Sometimes great discussions can happen organically, without any refereeing, but we've all endured enough bad meetings to know that isn't always the case.

The discussion is a lot like a ball on the soccer field. In an evenly matched game, it's going to be passed around a lot, moving back and forth between the sides. Sometimes the ball will go out of bounds and the ref will blow the whistle, bringing it back in bounds. The analogy breaks down, of course, because a discussion shouldn't be about scoring points or winning— hopefully everyone knows they're on the same team.

Anyway, the ref's job is to be objective, ensure a fair game, and keep the ball moving. That means watching the field closely and dealing with issues immediately. While that one ref who yellow carded my opponent was on top of the situation and prevented a fight, I've known plenty of refs that needed a pair of glasses.

The players that flout the rules may "like" oblivious refs that don't keep control; however, those refs certainly aren't respected. And they're hated by the players that try to follow the rules.

My point is that if you don't admit—and deal with—what is obvious to everyone else, you will appear oblivious. Just because everyone is too polite to tell the rambler to shut up, that doesn't mean they don't see it. They see it and are assuming that either you 1) are oblivious or 2) aren't brave enough to step up. Neither of those are good.

If you don't admit what's obvious, you appear oblivious.

Finally, a ref stays out of the game. They don't score points for one team or excessively penalize the other. Facilitating a meeting frequently means tempering your own opinions and thoughts for the sake of encouraging a more thoughtful discussion.

That said, here are some key "discussion infractions" that you need to watch for:

1. DOMINATING THE BALL.

Some people are more confident talking than others. Others talk too much to compensate for their lack of confidence. Whatever the reason, they hog the ball and prevent others from speaking.

Dealing with dominators requires a great deal of emotional intelligence—the people who are afraid of conflict usually do it the worst. If that's a "growth area" for you, I'd again encourage you to invest in improving your own emotional intelligence.

People who are afraid of conflict usually do it the worst.

In any case, be very careful about publicly correcting a dominator—you are likely to both deeply offend them and discourage others from talking. First, you can address them as part of a group, "I appreciate that perspective from the tech team. Do any of the designers want to weigh in?" Or, "I'd like to hear from some of you that haven't spoken yet." Second, try some subtle phrases like, "That's a great point. Let's find out what Luis thinks." Or, "Can you hang on to that thought for a moment?"

Hopefully, the dominator will take a hint. If not, try using the private chat (and triple check that it's private!). First, thank them for their input and then enlist their "help." For example, "Hey, good stuff, but I'm trying to get some of the quieter folks to speak up. Can you help me with that?" This technique works even better if you can personally chat with them prior to the meeting.

2. OUT OF BOUNDS

An equally common infraction is kicking the discussion out of bounds (AKA "rabbit trails"). This is one of my biggest pet peeves. One person says something that is a little off topic and then passes it to someone else who runs with it. Before you know it, there's a whole game taking place beyond the sidelines. The whole time, the facilitator is nodding and saying things like, "Good point. Interesting perspective." They're so eager to keep the discussion going they don't seem to notice how off topic it is.

Your job as a facilitator isn't to encourage discussion, but to encourage *productive* discussion. See why an agenda is so important? This is where courage comes in. You need the courage to say, "That's a great topic, but I want to respect everyone's time by keeping us on topic. Maybe we should set up another meeting for that?"

Your job isn't to encourage discussion, but to encourage productive discussion.

A quick clarification. There's a big difference between "off topic" and "offsides." In soccer, offsides is when someone on the offense gets ahead of the ball. Sometimes, someone will ask a question or make a comment about something you'll be covering later. In that case, say something like "That's a really great comment. In fact, we're going to be talking about that in a little bit. Can you do me a favor and put that in the chat box as a reminder?" This allows you to keep the ball moving (i.e., encourage continuing participation) without allowing the "players" to get ahead of the topic.

3. INTERRUPTIONS

In soccer, the referee is responsible to watch for reckless behavior or excessive force, such as tripping or charging their opponent. When that happens, they blow their whistle, take the ball away, and give it to the opponent for a free kick. Sometimes this requires making a judgment call. Was that a deliberate attack or were they going for the ball?

Discussions involve a certain amount of back and forth ("interjecting," from Chapter 5), so pay attention for when that crosses into interrupting and cutting others off. This is where it's extremely helpful to set out the expectations and ground rules in advance. For instance, if the rule is "Whoever has the floor, has the mic; everyone else must use the chat box," it's easy for you to know if someone has committed an infraction. In any case, there will be times that you must pause the conversation and return it to another player.

4. PERSONAL FOULS

We'll call this unsportsmanlike conduct. It can be things like bullying, excessive aggressiveness, unfair argument tactics, or ad hominem attacks (attacking the person instead of the argument). Basically, it's any behavior that creates an unsafe environment and shuts down discussion. This doesn't happen often, but this is where facilitators really earn their keep.

Stopping "unsportsmanlike conduct" is where facilitators really earn their keep.

These situations need to be dealt with immediately or else you risk losing all control. But if you're paying attention, you can frequently "nip it in the bud." This where the chat feature gives you a virtual advantage. A quick, respectful private message— one that assumes the best of the other person's motives—can frequently stop bad behavior before it becomes a problem. Something like, "Hey Jodi, I can tell that you're really passionate about this point, but you may need to tone it down a bit because that came across as kind of personal. Thanks!"

My rule of thumb is to keep it private if I can. But sometimes a comment is so public and over the top that I have to respond publicly. In those cases, I'll still be as respectful as possible and assume the best of their motives, while clearly stating their conduct was inappropriate. It's important to be as specific as possible. For instance, "I'm sorry Tony, but I have to interrupt you right there. I can tell this is really important to you, but we need to keep this respectful. Do you need a moment to regroup, or would you like to give that another shot?"

View that as a yellow card. They get one warning, then it's time to mute their mic or eject them from the meeting. And some-times—for especially disrespectful or inappropriate behavior—you have to give out a red card. I.e., boot them immediately. Fortunately, this kind of behavior is pretty rare, but it's important to understand that silence on your part will be viewed as consent. If you don't respond to something inappropriate, people will interpret that as agreement.

If you don't respond to something inappropriate, people will interpret that as agreement.

5. ENCOURAGING RELUCTANT SPEAKERS

I'm going to just stop with the soccer analogies while I'm still ahead. Another one of your key roles isn't just to control misguided or aggressive discussion, it's to encourage reluctant participants. Sometimes, the most insightful people are the least inclined to speak. Maybe they're introverts who need time to process everything. Or maybe they're literally too polite. As the facilitator, be mindful of those who haven't spoken and consider calling them by name. Something like, "Rick—you have a thoughtful look over there. Did you want to say something?" Also remind them they can use the chat box and, if they make a good observation there, ask them to elaborate "on air."

This is also a great place to make good use of long pauses. Ask the question then say, "I want to hear from someone who hasn't spoken yet," then just wait confidently while smiling. The awkward pause will practically force them to speak!

6. LACK OF DISAGREEMENT

Another thing to watch for is the echo chamber. Many people are too polite to disagree publicly with whatever has been said. It may be more comfortable to just nod along, but it costs everyone the benefit of divergent opinions.

Sometimes you, as the facilitator, need to get the ball rolling by respectfully playing the devil's advocate. I'm famous for the phrase, "Let me push back on that a little." It's a great way to gently contradict the prevailing view and create deeper discussion. It's your job to model respectful disagreement. I love the way Colin Powell put it:

> When we are debating an issue, loyalty means giving me your honest opinion, whether you think I'll like it or not. Disagreement, at this state, stimulates me. But once a decision is made, the debate ends. From that point on, loyalty means executing the decision as if it were your own.

That is the mindset I want to encourage in meetings.

It's your job to model respectful disagreement.

7. SIDE CONVERSATIONS AND ARGUMENTS.

We've all been there: what's supposed to be a group meeting becomes a conversation (or, worse, an argument) between two people as everyone else scrolls their media feed. And once they've picked up their phones, they might not put them back down! Once again, this is where you serve the rest of the participants. Politely step in and say something like, "It seems like you two should take this discussion offline. Can you circle back to us with your consensus?"

BREAKOUT ROOMS

The more people in a virtual meeting, the fewer who will speak out. This is true of all meetings but especially web conferencing. This is more than a numbers game (more people means less time per person). There's also a sociological component: the larger the crowd, the more confidence required for speaking up. But confidence doesn't necessarily equate to capability—YouTube is filled with viral videos of confident idiots!

The more people in a virtual meeting, the fewer who will speak out.

Breakout rooms allow you to overcome this dynamic and avoid groupthink by creating smaller discussion groups, leading to more and better participation. Some studies show that groups begin to lose their "team dynamic" around seven members, making breakout rooms vital for any truly participant-focused meeting that exceeds that size.[26]

That doesn't mean breakout rooms are only for participant-focused meetings. They are one of my favorite tools for presenter-focused meetings. Here are some effective ways you can use them:

- A quick, five-minute "side-bar" to change the pace and keep participants engaged.

- Emphasize a major point by giving participants a chance to interact and apply it to their own situation.

- Bring together existing teams (such as all the engineers) for a focused discussion.

- Encourage networking and personal connections.

---

[26] https://ir.uiowa.edu/cgi/viewcontent.cgi?article=3537&context=etd

Knowing how you want to use the breakout rooms, strategically schedule them throughout the meeting. For instance, if your goal is keeping participants engaged, I'd suggest spreading them evenly throughout your presentation, roughly every fifteen minutes.

How do you create breakout rooms? Each platform will be a little different, but here's a quick tutorial for Zoom (as of the time of publication), but other platforms are similar.

First, you'll need to enable breakout rooms. Log on to Zoom via the website (*not* the app). Go to "Settings" and scroll down to "Breakout room" and enable.

Now create a meeting as a host (you can only create breakout rooms if you're the host) and then click "Breakout Rooms":

From there, you'll be given options, like how many rooms to create and how to assign participants.

Again, how you assign people should be driven by your goals. You'll also be able to schedule the rooms and decide how long they should be.

The most important step, however, is giving very clear directions about what you *want* them to do and *how long* they have. And I mean very clear—unsupervised people in small groups are even more apt at wasting time than those in large groups. Then, as the host, be sure to circle through the rooms, making sure they understood the instructions, answering questions, and keeping everyone on track.

> ## Unsupervised people in small groups are even more apt at wasting time than those large in groups.

MISCELLANEOUS DISCUSSION TIPS

Here are some other tips to keep handy:

1. ALLOW FOR A NATURAL RHYTHM OF HEAVY AND LIGHT DISCUSSIONS.

Not everything needs to be down to business. Notice how many dramatic movies have a comedic character whose job is to keep things from staying too heavy for too long. So, if a small tangent about the price of lattes seems to provide a breather, don't squash it, but don't let it run for too long.

2. SCHEDULE BREAKS.

It's well known that taking breaks increases productivity. This is especially true when it comes to virtual meetings. [27] Long hours

---

[27] https://www.huffpost.com/entry/5-science-backed-ways-taking-a-break-boosts-our-productivity_b_8548292#:~:text=5%20Science-Backed%20Ways%20Taking%20a%20Break%20Boosts%20Our,Playing%20hard%20helps%20us%20with%20working%20hard.%20

staring at a computer screen without physical activity is well known for creating "Zoombies."[28] Don't meet longer than an hour without a ten-minute break.

As always, communicate the game plan with the participants. So, for a 90-minute meeting, let them know at the beginning that there will be a ten-minute break about halfway through. Doing so will minimize the number of people slipping away for an "unauthorized" break to use the bathroom, etc. Then give them a heads up a few minutes before. Saying something like, "Okay, let's finish up this point and then we'll take a ten-minute break," will give them that extra bit of incentive to dig in.

When giving breaks, give clear instructions about when to return and also encourage them to do some sort of physical activity. A sprint up and down the stairs can do wonders for one's creativity!

3. HAVE AN "ASSISTANT" WITH CO-HOSTING AUTHORITY.

If possible, and depending on the situation, having someone to help you manage the chat comments, presentation software, and various technical issues can help you focus on facilitating. For Zoom, have your "assistant" login early and assign them ability to Co-Host by clicking on the three dots next to their name in Gallery mode

---

[28] https://www.conferencesthatwork.com/index.php/event-design/2020/05/schedule-breaks-during-online-meetings/

4. PAY ATTENTION TO THEIR ATTENTION.

We've all had those teachers that didn't care if you drifted far off into la-la land, so long as you didn't interrupt them. In his book *The Seven Laws of the Learner*, Bruce Wilkinson said, "Teachers are responsible to cause students to learn." In the same way, you are responsible to keep the participants engaged. This is especially important in presenter-focused meetings where you're doing most of the talking. Actively monitor for cues that the participants are losing their attention. Ask questions, use online polls, and insert feedback sessions to break things up.

> ## You are responsible to keep the participants engaged.

4. KEEP USEFUL PHRASES NEARBY.

Here are a handful of phrases to keep handy:

"Please" and "Thank you." I know this seems painfully obvious, but if you, as the facilitator, are feeling under the gun, it's easy to forget the obvious.

"Allow me to be direct." Have you ever interacted with someone and initially thought them rude, only to later realize that they were friendly but didn't beat around the bush? This phrase says, "I respect you and your time, so I'm going to be honest" without seeming rude.

"Tell me more about that." A lot of people undervalue their own insights and hence cut themselves short. This both says, "I like what you said" and "I want to hear more."

"What do you think about that, _____?" By using their name, you solicit their participation.

"Have I answered your question?" We've all had the experience of asking a question, only to have it completely misunderstood. Most of the time, people are too embarrassed to clarify, but this question makes it easy to do so, while inviting follow-up questions.

"Can I get back to you on that? In fact, would you email me a reminder?" You aren't going to have all the answers and that's okay. If you don't know the answer, it's far better to do the research than to make up something that you'll regret. This is triply true of making a promise. Never agree to something while you're feeling under pressure. Asking them to email you both filters out flippant requests and also relieves you of the burden of remembering.

Never agree to something while you're feeling under pressure.

"Where does this fit in with…?" This is a great way to handle an apparently off-topic comment because it doesn't dismiss the idea but allows the participant to either acknowledge it's "off topic-edness" or connect it back to the main discussion.

"How do you think we should move forward?" Not only does this invite input, but it signals that it is time to stop talking and start *doing*.

If you faithfully utilize the material in this chapter, you'll be able to lead better meetings—virtual or in-person—than the majority of professionals out there. But maybe leading meetings is no sweat for you. It's the speaking part that frightens you. In the next chapter, we'll talk about embracing your fears and getting on path to becoming a great presenter, no matter what the format.

*Confidence allows our listeners to focus on
what we're saying instead of on us.*

Chapter 10:
Speak Like a Pro

Think about the last amazing speech you heard, like maybe a TED talk or an inspiring political speech. From almost the moment a capable speaker opens their mouth, you know you're in good hands. They exude confidence and authority.

Contrast that to some poor student giving their first speech in COMM 102. Your empathy kicked in and you felt embarrassed for them as they nearly hyperventilated. As a result, you were more focused on them than their speech.

Here's what I want you to notice: Confidence allows our listeners to focus on what we're saying instead of on us. Said another way, the less you worry about what the audience thinks about you, the less they'll think about you.

Confidence allows our listeners to focus on what we're saying instead of on us.

While this isn't strictly a public speaking book, your ability to speak with confidence is one of the most important keys to being a successful virtual presenter. In my book *Speak With No Fear*, I called public speaking a universal advantage—a skill that gives you an advantage in nearly any profession or situation.[29] No matter your job title, it increases your perceived authority and makes you more valuable in your organization. I believe that you cannot afford *not* to invest in your speaking abilities (but I am a little biased since I coach speakers and lead speaking workshops).

This chapter is no substitute for that investment, but confident speaking is too important not to address. Consider this a survey of the topics that you'll need to study later.

VIRTUAL ENGAGEMENT

In Chapter 2, I said that one of the key principles of virtual meetings is to treat it like real conversations. Likewise, you must learn to treat virtual presentations like real speeches. That seems obvious, but so many become someone else when the camera turns on. Exciting people become boring. Easygoing people become stiff. Kind people look rude.

You must learn to treat virtual presentations like real speeches.

As I said earlier, virtual engagements require an act of imagination. That means the camera (because you're looking at the camera, not your screen) becomes the actual audience that you're speaking to. I said "audience" not "person" because giving a presentation is not quite the same as a conversation.

---

[29] Speak With No Fear, 2nd ed. P. 18

Close, but not quite. There is more authority, a different cadence, a different attention to details, and a different stage presence.

Virtual Opportunity

Stepping out onto a stage in front of tens of thousands is enough to unsettle even the most experienced speaker. A room of that size just sounds and feels different. But with virtual meetings, it doesn't matter if you're talking to one or one million—you're still looking at a camera. That can give your nerves a real break, but don't get too comfortable. That's also a recipe for disaster.

PREPARATION, PREPARATION, PREPARATION

They say there are three keys to real estate: location, location, location. Similarly, there are three keys to public speaking: preparation, preparation, preparation:

1. PREPARE YOURSELF.

Study the art of public speaking. Join a Toastmasters group. Find ways to practice your speaking skills (such as clear articulation, hand gestures, and facial expressions). There are a few people who are naturally comfortable on stage (real or virtual), but the majority of us start out terrified—I once induced a psychosomatic fever to avoid a speech—but gain confidence through practice.

2. PREPARE YOUR MATERIAL.

There is no substitution for knowing your material inside and out. Nightmares about giving a speech in your underwear are your brain's attempt to grapple with your *inner* unpreparedness by manifesting it externally. Follow the iceberg principle of research: The content you share should just be the tip of everything you know about your topic. Only having enough to fill your notes will leave you feeling like…well, like you're only wearing underwear.

3. PREPARE YOUR PRESENTATION.

It's one thing to know your content, it's another to get it organized and ready to share. Since you've prepared more material than you can share, how do you know what to share and what to keep in your back pocket? By knowing your purpose. Just like we talked about in Chapter 5, you should be able to say, "My purpose for this presentation is _____" and that will determine your content.

Get that content onto paper then figure out the best way to organize it and make it interesting. Then turn it into an outline and practice giving your talk until you're completely comfortable with it. Then practice it in front of people you trust for good feedback. One of my *Speak With No Fear* principles is that the first time you give a speech should never be the first time you give that speech.

The first time you give a speech should never be the first time you give that speech.

CONTROL THE FEAR

Confidence is not the absence of fear but *fear under control*. Here the seven strategies from my book:

1. ***Uncover & Clean the Wound:*** Deal with any past speaking fears that are crippling you.

2. ***Imagine the Worst:*** Mentally prepare yourself for the worst-case scenario.

3. **You Be You:** Figure out how *you* speak, instead of trying to speak like someone else.

4. **Speak to One:** Connect with one person prior to speaking.

5. **It's Not About You:** Focus on serving your audience.

6. **Channel The Power:** Harness the power of fear to give you an edge.

7. **Be in the Moment:** Enjoy what you're doing and everyone else will enjoy it too.

Those are painfully abbreviated descriptions, but they're a good place to start.

SOME TECHNIQUES

Content is king. If you don't have anything worth sharing, these techniques will be nothing more than fluff—and audiences can see right through fluff. But if you've got the goods, these techniques will keep them engaged. As before, this is the highly abbreviated version.

- Vary your velocity and volume. Think of four quadrants: loud & slow, loud & fast, quiet & slow, quiet & fast. Move through these to add interest.

- Likewise, vary your pitch. Monotone is bad enough in person. In virtual communication, it's a death sentence.

- Use pauses—for emphasis, for variety, to connect with the audience, to breathe and think, to allow the listener to ponder.

- While we're at, be sure to breathe. Nervousness causes shallow breathing. Take deep, calming breaths to regain control.

- Stand to speak. As I explain in Chapter 12, I have a standing desk that allows me to stand for presentations, which gives me more lung capacity and hence more vocal power.

- If you must sit, keep both feet flat on the floor and sit up straight. This will improve your lung capacity and convey greater authority.

- Shift your posture (whether sitting or standing). Lean in to make a point, lean back to give the listener space to think.

- In Chapter 12, we'll talk about the "Rule of Thirds." Use that to pay attention to how you are framed by the camera.

- Use presentation tools to clarify the message, not complicate or distract from it.

- Talk with your hands—but only if it's natural for you. Better no gestures than gestures that look forced.

- Tell stories. Tell more stories. Our brains literally process stories differently and remember them better.

- Don't be afraid to use notes, in fact, doing so is easier and more discreet in virtual meetings.

- Finally, smile. This is my number one advice to clients. Smiling releases calming neurotransmitters, strengthens your voice, and connects you with others.

So, we covered starting strong, facilitating great interactions, and speaking with confidence. But sometimes, the real secret to great meetings lies in what happens after you log out. We'll cover that next.

Meetings without follow-up destroy initiative and cost credibility.

Chapter 11

Close the Meeting and Follow up

Have you ever been part of an amazing brainstorming meeting? Ideas were flowing, laughter was flying, and you left eager to be part of what was coming next—but then there was no follow-up and nothing changed. Meetings like that are *worse* than a waste of time. They destroy initiative and cost the leadership massive credibility.

Meetings without follow-up destroy initiative and cost credibility.

Too often, presenters and facilitators are so focused on just getting through the meeting—and so relieved to almost be done—that they don't think about how to conclude the speech. That's like a pilot heading into the cabin for a drink while still on the landing approach. You still must land that thing!

Almost as bad is finishing the meeting but failing to do any follow-up. That's like leaving the plane on the tarmac and not letting the passengers get off. So, let's look at how to land your virtual meeting and get the participants where they need to be.

MISSION ACCOMPLISHED?

The first question is *when* to end a meeting. Speaking in general terms, here are the goals that you need to accomplish for each type of meeting:

Informational: Did the necessary information get conveyed and was it understood? Do not ignore that last part.

Motivational: This may be harder to gauge, but ask if the participants were inspired and equipped to _____.

Persuasive: Have the participants been given a compelling reason to believe that doing/buying ____ is in their best interest, *and* have they been given a clear "Call to Action"?

Collaborative: Was groupthink banished and has the issue at hand been fully examined from every side? Have the conclusions been recorded and is there a solid plan for the next steps?

Executive: Have all the decisions been made and is there a solid plan for their execution?

Debriefing and Feedback: Has the event or product been fully examined, good and bad, and is there a plan for implementing the findings in the future?

Networking and Connections: Have the participants been able to find common interests, personally and professionally, and been given the tools to connect offline?

From these general goals, return to your meeting's purpose and the agenda. Have those been accomplished?

That done, here's the rule: A meeting should end when its objectives have been accomplished or it has reached its scheduled ending, *whichever comes first.*

A meeting should end when its objectives have been accomplished or it has reached its scheduled ending, whichever comes first.

I cannot overemphasize that last part. If you accomplish the objective in half the time, end it. No one will complain. But otherwise, always end a meeting on schedule even if the objectives haven't been accomplished. Why? Because meetings are like hot air—they expand or contract to fit the space given. Like my board meetings in Chapter 6, enforcing a time limit will improve efficiency.

Meetings are like hot air—they expand or contract to fit the space given.

There are, however, two important exceptions. First, brainstorming requires sufficient time to get the creative juices flowing. Sometimes, your best ideas come *after* you think it's all been figured out.

Second, an emergency will occasionally necessitate an extended executive meeting—sometimes you've gotta do what you've gotta do. But never forget how easily exceptions can become the rules.

WRAP IT UP WITH A BOW

When it's time to end, purposely close it with these three elements: 1) a summarizing closing statement, 2) clear next steps, and 3) grateful farewell.

I. SUMMARIZING CLOSING STATEMENT

There's a quote familiar to writers and speakers that applies to presenters as well, "Tell them what you're going to tell them, tell them, and tell them what you've told them."

> ### "Tell them what you're going to tell them, tell them, and tell them what you've told them."

It's not simply a matter of repetition:

"Tell them what you're going to tell them..." By sending out the agenda in advance, you get the participants into the right mental space to fully engage the content.

"...tell them..." This is the meeting itself.

"...and tell them what you've told them." Always end with a quick summary that ties it together with maximum brevity.

In the case of presenter-focused meetings, you have the advantage of knowing the content in advance so you can craft a brief closing statement that is so pithy that everyone will want to write it down.

In the case of participant-focused meetings, make notes as the meeting goes so that you can tie everything up at the end with a succinct statement that both honors the participants and also summarizes their thoughts.

Did you catch a theme here? Maximum brevity, brief, succinct. Keep the summary really short. Literally no more than a minute or two. There's nothing worse than thinking the meeting is over then having to endure a speech disguised as a summary. This is a proven way to make the participants mentally log off before you hit the next two crucial elements.

2. CLEAR NEXT STEPS

You probably noticed that the goals I gave for each type of meeting included some sort of action steps. No matter what kind of meeting you are leading, there is something that you want to *happen* afterwards. It is your job to end the meeting by making those next steps incredibly clear.

3. GRATEFUL FAREWELL.

Thank people for coming and mean it. I don't care if you paid them to be there, they still gave you a portion of their most valuable resource. After that, give them "permission" to log out, but offer to hang around for a little bit in case anyone has extra questions.

FOLLOW UP

You're almost done, but not quite. The last step is a written follow-up via email, Slack, or whatever interoffice tool you use. It doesn't need to be long—it *shouldn't* be long—just enough to remind everyone of the key ideas, the decisions made, and the action points (with assignments).

That last one is the secret to successful meetings: making sure everyone knows who is responsible to do what. By creating that accountability, you greatly improve the chances of the meeting accomplishing its objectives. In the case of persuasive meetings, this is a great place to provide another Call To Action.

> **By creating that accountability, you greatly improve the chances of the meeting accomplishing its objectives.**

One more thing: If you want to become a better presenter, include a short survey asking what they liked and what needs to be improved.

———————

The famous proverb "For the Want of a Nail," ends with "For want of a battle the kingdom was lost. And all for the want of a horseshoe nail." A kingdom is clearly more important than a nail, just as everything you've read so far is more important than "the technical stuff." But the technical stuff can ruin all your hard work, so that's what we'll hit next, starting with your set up.

PART FOUR: **SETTING UP**

A professional setup communicates authority.

Chapter 12:
Set Up for Success

We call this the digital age, but we might as well call it the visual age. Some readers might not even remember a time before selfies, back when you had to carefully consider each picture because of the cost of film and development. For better or worse, digital cameras (posing as smart phones) have given us a glimpse into everyone else's daily life.

The quality of these cameras have increased tremendously over the past ten years to where feature movies have been filmed on iPhones. Your next Zoom meeting doesn't need to be Oscar-nomination worthy, but the quality of your equipment and setup must—at a minimum—not detract from your message.

I trust you don't want to do the minimum.

Your setup reflects directly on your professionalism. A grainy picture in a poorly lit room communicates one thing. A sharp, well-lit picture communicates something else. In this chapter, we're going to focus on your equipment and how to set it up. In PR, they talk about "optics." Think of all this as "personal PR."

Your setup reflects directly on your professionalism.

VIRTUAL SETUP

Your virtual setup represents all the elements required for creating a professional space online:

1. Equipment (camera, mic, lighting, etc.)

2. Your physical location and backdrop

3. Software (web meeting platform, presentation software, apps like Kahoot, etc.)

Everything that you've been taught about the power of first impressions directly applies to your setup. The camera you use, the quality of your sound, and the look of your background will communicate something to everyone attending a virtual meeting with you.

Think about some of the online content you've seen. For instance, mentally compare an off-the-cuff rant, recorded on a phone by someone walking through a noisy mall versus a well-staged talk given by someone using a high-quality camera and mounted Yeti mic.

The former might be great for a motivational speaker giving a spontaneous "thought of the day" and, if you have an established platform as big as the Kardashians, you might be able to get away with that, but the rest of us need to give attention to our presentation. A professional setup communicates, "I know what I'm doing." It conveys authority and intentionality.

A professional setup communicates authority.

What do you want your virtual setup to communicate about you? Not everyone will have the same answer. It will be driven by your industries, your goals, and your audience. But you need to think through every aspect of your setup and what it says.

Find a way to record your next virtual meeting then watch it as if you were a potential client. Examine the crispness of the video, the clarity of the audio, the noise in the background, the impression your backdrop makes, etc. Would you hire you?

INVESTING IN YOUR FUTURE

Do you remember your first job that required nicer clothes? Going from a California nonprofit, where shorts were the norm, to a consultative sales position in the northwest meant I had to buy a new wardrobe. It was no small expense, but I understood it to be the cost of doing business.

I think it's funny that some people will be excited to find a suit jacket for "only" $400 but balk when I tell them to buy a $40 camera for virtual meetings. "What's wrong with the one on my computer?" they ask. I try to help them see that their setup is simply another expense, just like their outfit. Equipment is the wardrobe of the modern era.

Equipment is the wardrobe of the modern era.

You need to be willing to make an investment in your setup. In this new age of virtual communication, your virtual setup has become part of your tools of the trade. Just like a painter needs good paint brushes, you need a good camera. Just like a chef needs no-slip shoes, you need a stand that puts your computer at eye level.

That's the bad news. The good news is that it doesn't need to be expensive. In fact, you can build a solid virtual setup for less than $150. While your specific situation may change things a little, here are the key things you need to invest in. You don't have to spend it all at once. As you read through this, think through which items are the highest priority.

Below, you'll find some of my recommendations, with prices (current as of time of publishing), or you can visit content.mikeacker.com for a pdf with links.

I. CAMERA

This is typically the first place where you'd want to spend money because it makes the most dramatic improvement. I had one client whose job required a lot of online presentations and realized how much more professional a great camera would make her look. So, she invested in the $200 camera I recommended (the Logitech BRIO webcam) and the difference was unbelievable. More expensive cameras don't just have more features but also better lenses, which is key (even when movies are filmed on an iPhone, they frequently attach a special lens).

If you don't have that much to spend, there are a lot of great cameras under $50. My personal rule of thumb is to look for cameras that have 1,000 plus reviews and 4.5 stars. However, make sure you dig into the reviews a little bit. Read some of the lower star reviews. They might bring an issue to light that would be a problem for you—like not being compatible with your computer.

Most cameras clip atop your screen, but your setup may require some sort of mount. You can find good gooseneck mounts for around $25. The advantage of these is extreme flexibility in the positioning of your camera. The disadvantage is that they are more prone to vibrations than a tripod and even typing could make the camera shake—something the other participants really want you to avoid!

Also, if you're using virtual communications for giving professional presentations or leading webinars, you can consider using multiple cameras and occasionally switching the angle to maintain interest. You can make it as elaborate (and expensive) as you like, but start small by plugging a second camera into your computer and switching on the fly by selecting alternating cameras in your web conferencing platform's settings. I use a total of three separate cameras, the Blackmagic ATEM Mini Pro (switching board) and powered webcam converters, which give my virtual keynotes a very high-end feel.

2. LIGHTING

The second most important element of your setup is lighting. Dimly lit rooms look unprofessional. The wrong shade of white can make you look sickly. There are some low-cost hacks you can use, such as a well-placed lamp or setting up in front of a window for natural light.

My current setup uses four $100 lights (Neewer Metal 10.6 inches Round LED Video Light with Stand) and two $75 ceiling mounted softbox studio lights. LED means less electricity and lower temperature (which matters when there are six of them!). On the Neewer style lights, among others, you can change the color from cold white to a warmer white.

The reason I need so much lighting is because I use my entire office as a studio and move around during virtual speaking engagements. If you're planning to stay in one spot, you don't need nearly that much lighting. The Lume Cube Video Conference Lighting Kit ($70) is a great option. There are many good lighting options in the $20 to $40 range.

As you set up your lights, the goal is evenly distributed light that doesn't wash you out. Experiment until you achieve the best results. Depending on your room, you may also need to invest in some blackout curtains ($20). Some can also help with outside noises.

Ergo-tip

Don't place your lights right next to the camera and avoid camera/lights combos. Otherwise, you'll effectively spend the entire meeting staring into a light. That's hard on the eyes and mentally fatiguing.

---

3. MIC

Arguably more important than your camera, is your microphone. Conducting an online meeting without video is frustrating; conducting it without audio is pointless. Your microphone affects the quality and tone of your voice, which can impact how you are perceived—would you rather sound more like Morgan Freeman or Meryl Streep, or like Mickey or Minnie Mouse? Additionally, your mic will affect how much ambient noise will be heard by other participants.

There is no right option for your mic setup—it depends on your usage. The Yeti mic is very popular, and for good reasons. When used with a pop filter and earbuds/headphones, it has great sound quality. Because of its low frequency capabilities, it will make your voice sound richer and more authoritative. It also has a very professional look, very similar to a radio studio. On the downside, it restricts your ability to move around. And they run around $150.

Though I use the Yeti mic, I'm also a fan of the FIFINE Studio Condenser USB Microphone. At $60, it's not only affordable but works great and comes with a professional stand.

Another option is a full headset (headphone/mic combo), like the Logitech USB Headset H390 ($25). It has a noise-cancelling mic and good clarity.

While we're talking about headsets: I personally don't use them because of the look I'm trying to achieve, especially when I'm doing a keynote speech. As much as possible, I want my participants to forget that I'm not physically present and headsets draw attention to that fact (have you ever attended a speech given by a person wearing a large headset?).

That said, headsets may be a great option for you, especially if you're working in a noisy environment—kids playing and dogs barking in the background isn't exactly professional. And I'll frequently use AirPods for quick, informal meetings with longstanding clients or vendors in a coffee shop—but never for an initial consultation with a prospective client!

4. DESK OR COMPUTER STAND

As I said earlier, you need to treat your camera as if it were the eyes of the other participants, so it needs to be mounted right above your screen so you can look at it and then easily glance down at their faces. I also talked about how important it is for the camera to be at eye level for you. Depending on your setup, that may require some repositioning of your computer. An adjustable computer stand can be an inexpensive option, usually around $20. However, using one of these may necessitate a Bluetooth keyboard and mouse so that you can continue working on your computer even as it is raised up off the desk ($40).

A more expensive option is a standup desk. Mine is a Flexispot Electric adjustable desk (around $250), which allows me to raise and lower my desk with a single button, and allows me to take advantage of the power of standing.

THE POWER OF STANDING

Have you ever seen an opera singer perform from a stool? To sing with that much power requires using full lung capacity. Go ahead and try it out: Take as deep of a breath as possible from the sitting position then again standing.

When it comes to public speaking, breath is power. When I give my presentations from a standing position, I have more strength, more control over my voice, and better presence.

Breath is power.

While we're at it, controlled breathing is one of the key tactics in *Speak With No Fear*. Taking time to breathe deeply calms you from the inside out. Pause for a breath is a powerful rhetorical device. And studies show that deep breathing is correlated with peacefulness, stillness, and calmness. Conversely, short breaths are characteristic of panic attacks.

And breathing is much easier standing up.

You don't need to be standing for every meeting, but it's well worth considering whenever you give a presentation. Give it a shot, what do you have to lose?

5. BACKGROUND

Following the 9/11 attack on America, President George W. Bush addressed the nation from the Oval Office. The President sat at a large desk, clear except for two leather binders. Behind him were a couple of family photos and he was flanked on either side by the American and Presidential flag. As Bush spoke, the camera tightened, showing only him from the shoulders up, the red and white stripes of the U.S. flag on one side and the eagle's talon, full of arrows, on the other. For the speech's entire four minutes, those symbols of war silently dominated the shot.

Regardless of your thoughts on what happened following 9/11, the intentionality was clear. America was responding with defiance.

You may never have to address a nation at such a pivotal moment, but you can still learn to intentionally craft your background.

Look at it this way. If you knew that your CEO or a potential client were going to visit your office, would you take some time to clean up? Maybe carefully select a project to leave on your desk and peek at the books on your bookshelf. If you were uncertain of his political stance, you might tuck away the political comics. In short, you'd look at your office with the eyes of an outsider and consider what it communicates.

The camera's view is effectively your virtual office. What does your office say about you?

The camera's view is effectively your virtual office.

Use these two principles for designing your background:

First, your background shouldn't be distracting. It shouldn't pull people's attention away from you or the meeting. Here are some suggestions:

- Make sure everything is clean and uncluttered. If you think it might be too busy, it probably is.

- Keep it organized: Many people (especially those with ADHD) will struggle if it's disorderly.

- Avoid distracting conversation pieces: A life-size Chewbacca Lego sculpture may be cool, but you don't want people focused on it instead of you.

- Avoid controversial items. Whether they're political or religious in nature, they may cause your audience to make snap judgments.

Second, your background should say something about you. You want to convey professionalism and authority:

- Have a specifically designed spot that says, "This is my job, and I take it seriously." A blank white wall or a view of your closet does not.

- Tasteful decorations will demonstrate your savvy. If décor isn't your thing, find someone who can help.

- Make the decorations compatible with your area of expertise but keep it subtle. Showiness can be a huge turn-off.

- Also consider items that demonstrate authority—if you're a pop culture guru, that Lego Chewbacca may not be such a bad idea.

Your background should convey professionalism and authority.

For my usual set up, I have a background of distressed wood that serves to frame me, some live plants, and a simple bookshelf with my best-selling books visible next to my Patrick Lencioni collection.

Virtual Opportunity

Virtual communication allows you to *construct* the reality you want to present. Some creative design can give you a more professional-looking office. Little tricks can be used to hide a physical feature that's always made you self-conscience. Displaying your notes on the screen like a teleprompter can make it look like you're working from memory.

The point is that virtual communication opens up a whole new bag of tricks that you can use to increase your authority and influence!

Maybe you're thinking, "No worries, Mike. I just use a virtual background." There are varying opinions on those, but I'm not a fan for several reasons. First, they only semi-satisfy the first principle of not being distracting, but don't say much about you and feel less authentic.

Second, humans are naturally suspicious. When I see a virtual background, I wonder what they're hiding and what's *really* in the background!

Third, the technology is not perfect. You can always tell when a person is using it, especially when they move. Gesture too quickly with your hand and it will temporarily disappear. Now *that's* distracting!

Basically, I only recommend a virtual background as the lesser of two evils. If you need to use one, here are some suggestions:

- Choose your background picture carefully. Make sure it's professional and not distracting.

- Use good lighting, which will help the "green screen" technology work better.

- Test the outfit you're planning to wear.

- Practice not moving too quickly.

60 Second Fix

Google "Zoom meetings" and skim the images, focusing only on participant's' backgrounds—real or virtual. What did you like and dislike?

6. FRAMING THE SHOT

I recently led a workshop on virtual communication for over 100 designers at Adobe, and it was a little nerve-racking when I got to the part of framing the shot. They're the experts on this stuff! I could just say, "rule of thirds" and they knew exactly what I meant.

Basically, the rule of thirds is a principle that photographers and videographers use to frame shots that create visual interest and is more pleasing to the eye.

Here's how it works. Imagine drawing a tic-tac-toe board across this image, dividing it into nine equal sections. The four points where the two horizontal and vertical lines intersect create your strongest focal points, then the lines themselves create the second strongest focal points. Rather than just centering the camera on the subject, try to make use of those focal points. Notice in the below picture that the child's head is at the top right intersection. His body follows the left vertical line and the top left intersection meets between his eyes.

How does this apply to your set up? In addition to setting the camera at eye level, you want to pay attention to how your "picture"—what the other participants see—is framed. Many cameras have a feature to add a "rule of thirds" grid. Turn it on and play with how to frame yourself. Try keeping your eyes at the top line, then experiment with moving to the left and right. What objects in your background line up with the focal points and create interest? (Note that in my standing set up my eyes are at the top line and my bookshelf and elbows are on the bottom third.)

The added benefit of keeping your eyes at the top line is that it keeps you a proper distance from the camera. You don't want to be any closer or else it will feel like you're intruding into the participants' personal space, which is emotionally taxing on them. But you don't want to be any further than that either. This positioning also visibly displays your shoulder's full range of motion. That's more important than you think because we communicate a lot with our shoulders.

60 Second Fix

Google "Zoom meetings" again, but this time pay attention to how the shots are framed. Which ones "felt" better? Can you see the rule of thirds at work?

As I've already said, those first five minutes are precious, and you can't afford to burn through them while you:

- Figure out your microphone.

- Make small talk.

- Edit your slides.

- Load up presentation software.

- Move to a different room or change computers for better connection.

_____

The next chapter looks at things that can make or break your presentation, like software and connectivity. Then I'll show you how to do a practice call that will tie everything from Chapters 12 and 13 together.

Never head into your big presentation without a full-dress rehearsal.

Chapter 13

Pick the Right Tools

Using a computer as an analogy, everything in the last chapter could loosely be compared to the hardware. Now we're going to focus on the software (metaphorically and literally). We'll start with the platform—the services that facilitate your virtual meetings. Then we'll look at presentation software—tools for going beyond just showing your face.

While this is written from the perspective of helping you choose which tools to use, it also serves as a good survey of the options. You'll probably need to have a working knowledge of more than one system.

VIRTUAL COMMUNICATION PLATFORMS BASICS

There seems to be no end of virtual communication software and platforms, each of them designed for different types of users. Before you choose one, you need to understand your own needs. Here are the key elements to keep in mind:

Availability: Make sure that everyone you want at your meeting can use the platform. For example, Facetime is the most used video conference platform, however it only works on Apple products.

A good rule of thumb is to use the most popular platform that does the job. Most people have at least a mild resistance to change and may choose to skip rather than learn a new program. Even having to create a new password is a sufficient barrier to many.

> ## Most people have at least a mild resistance to change and may choose to skip rather than learn a new program.

Ease of use: Some platforms are more intuitive than others. Facebook Messenger is the second most used platform because it's easy to use. But "easy to use" frequently means fewer options.

Reputation: What a platform promises and what it delivers may not be the same thing. Research the company's reputation for things like:

- Connectivity and reliability: Do they have much down time?

- Customer service: Free services may have nothing more than a "knowledge base." Others offer 24/7 service.

- Security: Do they keep your data safe? Will they protect you from "Zoom bombing"?

Limitations: How many people can meet? How long can the meetings last? This is directly related to the next item.

Cost: Many services have a free version, but with greater limitations and fewer features. Don't start using a free platform that you wouldn't be willing to pay for if you outgrow the free version. If you don't think about the future, you'll either be stuck using something that doesn't grow with you or you'll have to change platforms, which will cost you and your team valuable time, potentially making the free service cost more in the long run.

Features: Have a clear idea of what features you need. If all you plan to do are short one-on-one coaching calls, the free version of Zoom will probably be fine—but not if you're hosting an all-day webinar for a thousand people. Here are some of the key features to look for:

- iPhone/Android apps

- Chat tools

- Document and file sharing

- Presentation tools

- Dial-in option, which provide more reliable audio and accessibility for those without great internet access

- Ability to record and transcribe the meeting

- Integration with popular tools like Google Docs and Office 365

- Ability to use prerecorded and live videos

- Scheduling tools

- Breakout rooms

SURVEY OF PLATFORMS

Among a seemingly endless variety of platforms, this will provide a quick look at some of the most popular and important options. I've grouped them into five categories, but in reality, there is much bleed over between them. You'll likely need to be comfortable working with several of these, based on the situation.

For more information about these platforms, visit my resource page content.mikeacker.com.

I. PERSONAL COMMUNICATION:

Platforms like *Facetime, Facebook Messenger, Google Duo, Google Hangouts, WhatsApp*, and *Marco Polo* are all popular and easy-to-use virtual communication platforms that utilize video in some form or another. While they represent the lion's share of online communication, they are best reserved for personal, rather than professional, communication. [30] Not only

---

[30] According to one survey, Facetime was used by 47.6% of adults in the US during the COVID-19 pandemic, Facebook Messenger 44.1%, WhatsApp 18.4%, Google Duo 14%, and Google Hangouts 8.6%. https://financesonline.com/video-web-conferencing-statistics

do they lack key features and have significant limitations, they also don't convey professionalism. Asking a potential client to Marco Polo you can be the equivalent of using "teamcullen 4ever91@yahoo.com" as your work email address.

> **Asking a potential client to Marco Polo you can be the equivalent of using "teamcullen4ever91@yahoo.com" as your work email address.**

Save these platforms for informal chats with friends and well-established clients. Important exception: Facebook Live has great potential for webinars (see below).

2. VIRTUAL MEETINGS

These are your standard virtual meeting and web conferencing platforms.

Zoom is the best known and most popular platform of this type. It is (literally) synonymous with video conferencing. For good reason too—relatively easy to use, a great free plan, good performance record, and plenty of features, including scheduling tools, breakout rooms, chat boxes, and a ceiling of 50,000 participants.

No less important, it is web-based and hence accessible on any device. And its popularity means that most people know how to use it. There may be other platforms out there with more features or cheaper plans, but if Zoom works for you, I'd recommend sticking with it.

Skype rests between personal communication and this category. It's been a lot around longer than Zoom and a lot of people already have personal accounts, making it familiar for many. Many of its services are free, but it's been known to suffer from buffering and delay problems.

GoToMeeting is another popular option and is considered by some to be the best option for small businesses. It has a lot of features, works on almost any device, but does not have a free version.

3. PLATFORM SPECIFIC

If your team uses G Suite and are comfortable with its tools, Google Meet may be a good option for you. Participants do not need to be G Suite subscribers, but they will need to sign in with a Gmail account.

Likewise, Office 365 subscribers may want to use *Microsoft Teams* for their virtual communication. It also allows guest participants. Given Microsoft's large presence in the workplace, it's not surprising that Teams is one of the most used virtual communication platforms.

4. INTERNAL COMMUNICATION

Slack is perhaps the best-known platform for communication within a company. *RingCentral Meetings* is becoming more popular, especially because of its generous free plan.

5. WEBINARS AND CONFERENCES

Facebook Live has been used effectively by a lot of entrepreneurs for hosting webinars. It's free, easily accessible for Facebook users, and you can attract customers via Facebook's paid advertising.

ClickMeeting is a popular choice for small businesses. It's more professional than Facebook Live and has a lot more features but does not have a free option. *ON24* is also highly rated and has a free trial.

Again, that is just a brief survey of an ever-changing landscape. Websites like TrustRadius and PCMag can help you navigate the choices or visit content.mikeacker.com for more details on the platforms available during the time of publishing. Just take the time to assess your current and future needs and review the options before making a decision.

VISUAL AIDS AND PRESENTATION SOFTWARE

Can we all agree that watching someone *just* talk can become boring? Effectively used visual aids, such as pictures, graphs, bullet points, and video clips do more than keep things interesting and engaging, they enhance your impact.

Watching someone just talk is boring.

"Effectively used" is crucial. Poorly used visual aids will actually be detrimental. They may distract from your content, unintentionally offend your audience, or undermine your authority. I once watched a chaplain introduce his opening devotional with a video clip of the dance rehearsal from *Flashdance*. What did that have to do with his devotional? Absolutely nothing. Michael Scott from *The Office* couldn't have pulled off a more enjoyable train wreck of awkwardness.

Here are some guiding principles that may help you avoid being someone else's illustration of poorly used visual aids:

I. KEEP IT RELEVANT AND PURPOSEFUL.

Every picture, text, or clip must have a reason for being used. Don't show pictures from your family's vacation to Cancun unless it directly applies to your presentation. Even after you've created your slides, go back through them and ask, one by one, "Does this actively contribute to my point?"

Here are some effective ways to use visual aids:

- Use a statistic to create interest or demonstrate a problem that needs to be fixed.

- Make an emotional impact with a picture, clip, or quote.

- Appeal to an authority via a quote.

- Distill key ideas into well crafted, memorable statements.

2. MAKE SURE IT'S INTERESTING.

Just because it's true doesn't mean that it's interesting. And just because it's interesting to you, doesn't mean it's interesting to everyone else. If past history suggests that you tend to ramble on about details that bore others, it may be a good idea to run your presentation past a friend or colleague.

> ## Just because it's true doesn't mean that it's interesting.

3. STAY CURRENT.

If your presentation uses that classic dark-blue fading to black background and yellow bullets shaped like this ❖, then you've just loudly proclaimed that you're still in 1998. It would be better not to have any visual aids at all than use ones that diminish your authority. You don't have to be cutting edge, but don't be dated.

You don't have to be cutting edge, but don't be dated.

4. IF IN DOUBT, DON'T.

Always keep your audience in mind when creating your presentation—you can get away with more when talking to a bunch of bartenders than to your daughter's third grade class. But steer clear of anything that could be interpreted as sexist, racists, or otherwise derogatory to any group. Be extra careful when referencing any group that you're not a part of, especially if you disagree with that group. Politically-charged jokes may get you a laugh or two but risk demolishing your credibility. When in doubt, don't use it. People lose their jobs because "people can't take a joke."

5. VISUAL AIDS SHOULDN'T BE THE FOCUS.

Visual aids are supplementary, not primary. Often, presenters rely too heavily on the visuals which effectively diminishes their authority. Use them to bring focus to you, because you carry the message—not the other way around. And don't forget Murphy's Law. If it can go wrong, it will. You should never be so reliant on the visual aids that their absence would throw you for a loop.

SURVEY OF PRESENTATION SOFTWARE

Having the content for a presentation is one thing, being able to put it all together without wanting to toss your computer across the room is another. Fortunately, presentation software has become far more intuitive over the years. And many of the virtual communication platforms have built-in tools, though they may lack features you need. Here are things to consider as you select your presentation software:

Ease of use: Is it intuitive or is there a huge learning curve? If you only plan on creating one or two presentations, it's probably not worth investing a lot of time learning a new program.

Compatibility and accessibility: Will the presentations you create be compatible with the platform you'll be using? And will you be able to save them and use them with another software in the future?

Features: Does it do what you want it to do?

Cost: As before, free software may end up costing you more in the long run. I don't know about you, but I hate sinking a lot of time into a program only to discover that it doesn't have some features I needed. The time wasted was more valuable than the cost of better software.

That said, here are the most popular presentation software:

PowerPoint is easily the best-known presentation software and has many great features. It's user friendly, especially if you're already comfortable with Microsoft's Office 365. But some users feel overwhelmed by the number of features.

Google Slides is the G Suite version of PowerPoint and has similar features. Both offer free and paid versions and there's a lot of debate online about which is best. One key difference is that Office 365 is largely desktop driven and G Suite is cloud based. In the end, I'd stick with whichever system (Office or G Suite) that you're already comfortable with.

Keynote is Apple's presentation software and is included on most of their devices. It's easy to use, especially for people already familiar with Apple. However, it lacks PowerPoint's compatibility and is not easily used on other systems.

Prezi is my personal favorite. With all of the above options, the presentation will take up the majority of the screen and you'll be stuck in a little box. But Prezi allows me to share the screen with it sitting over my shoulder as I continue making eye contact with the participants. Additionally, it's basic format is completely different. Whereas PowerPoint and Slides are linear—proceeding through a series of slides—Prezi is non-linear. It's more like moving around a map, zooming in and out as needed. Some people love the creative freedom this offers, but others find it confusing. And poorly designed presentations can leave people feeling carsick.

As with the platforms, take the time to consider your current and future needs. Don't rush to one software until you've played around with the options.

CONNECTIVITY

The final area to check is your connectivity. Nothing screams "I'm not prepared!" like a bad connection. Stuttering speech, lagging video, and being dropped from the meeting kills communication and wastes time.

Nothing screams "I'm not prepared!" like a bad connection.

The amount of bandwidth you need varies, but Zoom recommends upload and download bandwidth of 1.2 megabits per second for one-on-one, 720p video calls and 1.8Mbps for full HD (1080p). A gallery-view meeting requires slightly more and Microsoft Teams' requirements are similar. Most networks easily offer those speeds, but you can use speedtest.net to check your bandwidth.

If you're going to be working from someone else's network, be sure to test it in advance. And not just once, but multiple times and under similar conditions as when your meeting will occur (i.e., the number of users on the network). It's like planning your travel time to the airport—don't base it on 3:00 a.m. traffic flow if you'll be going during rush hour. If you're not convinced there will be sufficient bandwidth, make other arrangements.

It's always wise to have a backup plan, especially for critical meetings. Using your cell phone as a hot spot can be a good option, but make sure you have good reception and sufficient data.

It's always wise to have a backup plan.

The same is true if you'll be on your home network. Test it well in advance and use speedtest.net to check your bandwidth. If the results are consistently lower than promised by your Internet Service Provider (ISP), then you may want to contact them.

If your bandwidth seems sufficient but you're still experiencing lag or connectivity problems, here are some things to check:

HOW MANY PEOPLE ARE ON THE NETWORK?

The other activity on your network will directly impact how much is left for you. So even if your service provider says you're getting 20Mbps, the other five people could be using it all up and not leaving enough for you. Don't forget that every single device (computer, phones, tablets, TV's, even appliances) connected to your network will take bandwidth. Your Wi-Fi router should allow you to check and see how many devices are connected and how much data they're using. And it goes without saying that you need to have a good password on your network to prevent any "freeloaders."

That to say, you may need to turn off some devices and ask others to refrain from bandwidth-hogging activities during your meetings to preserve your bandwidth.

DO YOU HAVE TOO MANY OTHER APPS OPEN?

Depending on your equipment's age and power, other apps may be causing your computer to slow down. Check Activity Monitor (Apple) or Task Manager (PC) to assess your computer's power usage (similar apps are available for Android and iPhone). If it looks like your system's memory is being taxed, shut down unnecessary apps.

USE A LAN OR TEST YOUR WI-FI CONNECTION

If at all possible, use a wired connection (LAN or Local Area Network) instead of Wi-Fi. My computer is directly plugged into the internet modem, giving me the best and fastest internet access in my house.

If that's not an option, be sure to test your connection because all the bandwidth in the world won't do you any good if your Wi-Fi signal is weak. And it isn't enough to see how many "bars" you have. Tools like repeaters are notorious for a lot of signal but with little data.

TROUBLESHOOTING YOUR CONNECTION

At some point, you may need to call a professional, but many problems can be fixed with a little patience and a lot of google searches. I'm not a computer tech, but here's how to perform basic troubleshooting:

In the words of Roy and Moss from *The IT Crowd*, did you try turning it off and on again? Always begin with resetting all components, including your modem and router, by turning them off for ten seconds and then restarting it. Just make you check with everyone else first—you don't want to be responsible for the loss of your daughter's Minecraft creation.

Did you try turning it off and on again?

From there, try to isolate the problem by eliminating every potential issue. Plug directly into the network (to eliminate any questions about Wi-Fi) and ensure everyone is off the network. If you have a good connection, try using Wi-Fi, but sit next to the router. Then move your device to its normal location. If it's still working fine, then let everyone else use the network and try again.

PRACTICE CALL

My friend, Josh, ran sound for his small college. As they were gearing up for their big "Open Campus" event, he realized they needed a new piece of equipment to handle the increased audio demand. Due to shipping delays, he got it the night before and stayed up late installing it. He ran a few tests and was satisfied with the results, even though he hadn't been able to try it out with the full band.

The next morning, the band struck up their dramatic opening only to fill the room with painfully distorted screeching. The audience literally covered their ears and everyone on stage, including the college president, glared at him. There was literally nothing he could do and he ducked out of sight in embarrassment. I asked him what happened next, and he said he blocked it all out. I don't think he was joking.

The following day, the president was surprisingly gracious. "We shouldn't have let you change the horse on the day of the race," he said. That's a lesson he has never forgotten and we would be wise to learn from his mistake.

Never head into your big presentation without a full-dress rehearsal. Once you've got your set up all done—good equipment, a background that says, "I'm a professional," a well framed shot, and plenty of bandwidth—it's time to make some practice calls.

Never head into your big presentation without a full-dress rehearsal.

Find a friend or colleague who is familiar with whatever platform you'll be using and ask them to attend a practice meeting. Be sure to mimic every aspect of the presentation as closely as possible and pay attention to these details:

- Do you know how to use every piece of equipment without thinking about it?

- Does the equipment work together seamlessly?

- Do you know how to start/join the meeting on this platform?

- Are you comfortable with every presentation software you might use?

- Are there any materials or information you need to have easily accessible?

Virtual Opportunity

In my book *Speak With No Fear*, I tell about a friend whose entire speech was shipwrecked because his fly was down. Online meetings allow you to monitor yourself and ensure that your gestures and facial expressions are communicating what you want them to—and to help you avoid wardrobe malfunctions.

Ask your friend to pay attention to these details:

- Did everything work properly?

- Did you appear confident with the platform and presentation material?

- Was the camera clear? Was there good lighting that didn't wash you out?

- Did you appear to look them in the eye without staring?

- How was the sound quality? Could they hear any background noises?

- Was your background non-distracting (good)? Was it professional (better)? Did it communicate your authority (best)?

- Were you framed well on the screen?

Don't get frustrated if everything doesn't come together the first time. That's why you're practicing! Repeat this with a new audience until you're completely comfortable with everything.

The right perspective, preparing yourself, courageous leadership, the right set up…we've covered a lot of ground. I believe I've given you all the tools you'll need to take you and your company to the next level of virtual communication

Companies that can embrace new technology without losing their core have the best shot at succeeding.

Chapter 14:
Conclusion

The Greek philosopher Socrates said this about the invention of writing:

> They will cease to exercise memory because they rely on that which is written, calling things to remembrance no longer from within themselves, but by means of external marks.

This irony is, of course, that the only reason we can quote him is because it was written down. But he wasn't wrong and science has only demonstrated that using smart phones and other technology has only increased our tendency to offload information. We remember less because we keep it stored somewhere. But, as the flood of information, ideas, and stories has only gotten bigger, writing has allowed us to collect and retain far more than would have been possible with oral tradition alone.

Like writing, virtual communication hasn't replaced face-to-face communication, but it instead offers another tool. And as with cars, computers, the internet, or any of the other great disruptors that were initially dismissed as mere novelties, virtual communication is here to stay and the companies that can embrace new technology without losing their core have the best shot at succeeding.

Companies that can embrace new technology without losing their core have the best shot at succeeding.

COVID-19 changed the world in many ways, some good and some bad. I believe that the explosion of Zoom and other web conferencing tools is in the "good change" category. As more and more people have become comfortable with virtual communication, my reach has mushroomed. No longer am I limited to working with techies and early adopters. CEOs are now just as prone to ask, "Can we Zoom?" as anyone else. My clientele can come from almost any nation on the face of the earth.

But it hasn't been easy. I've had to learn how to speak through the door to take full advantage of these opportunities. That has been my purpose for this book: to help you maximize the benefits of virtual communication while minimizing the drawbacks.

The four sections of this book represent the key concepts that you must not only master but teach to your team:

1. ENGAGE

We must switch from solo mode to social mode and engage others as real people, treating them with the same courtesies we'd offer face-to-face. Look them in the eye (via the camera) and give them our full attention. But it's not *just* like face-to-face. We must use extra energy to push ourselves through the screen, and we will receive more energy back in return to the extent of leaving our meetings more refreshed.

2. ATTEND

By giving more to the meetings we attend, including preparing ourselves and dressing for the occasion, we will get more benefit from them. Special attention needs to be paid to how we present ourselves, so we can be mindful of how we'll be perceived by others.

3. LEAD

Great meetings are the result of great leadership. It starts by proper preparation: having an agenda, carefully selecting the participants, knowing what type of meeting it is, and communicating expectations. But facilitators really prove their mettle during the meeting by keeping things on track for the benefit of the entire group.

4. SET UP

Our virtual set up—everything the participants can see or hear—reflects on our professionalism. That's far too important to leave to chance. It's vital to think through and test every element to make sure it works as desired.

Nothing in this book is impossible and some of it is exceedingly simple—like wearing pants to your next Zoom meeting. But some of it will take work and some of it will take some courage.

It will be worth it.

All the energy you put into virtual meetings will be paid back, with interest, as your meetings become more engaging, more, empowering, and more productive. It's a small investment that will pay off in ways you can't imagine.

ABOUT MIKE ACKER

Mike Acker is a keynote speaker, author, executive, and communication coach with over twenty years of speaking, leadership development, and organizational management experience.

Beyond corporate training, Mike engages in his community as a Seattle TEDx speaker coach and works with international agencies to provide relief amidst poverty.

Mike also enjoys rock-climbing, wake surfing, skiing, church, building Legos with his son Paxton, and going on dates with his wife Taylor. Mike believes in the power of prayer, exercise, journaling, and real community to counter the stresses of everyday life.

http://www.mikeacker.com

SHARE WITH OTHERS

Can you help? If you liked this book and found it helpful, could you please take a brief moment to review it on Amazon? This effectively helps you *share* the book with others.

Simply visit https://www.amazon.com/author/mikeacker and select *Speak & Meet Virtually*. Then leave your honest feedback!

Reviews are extremely important to the success of a book! So, if you like what you've read (or even if you didn't), then please take two minutes to help me out with a review.

THANK YOU.

I appreciate your feedback! And if you want to stay connected, sign up for my email list.

https://subscribe.stepstoadvance.com/me

Explore The Public Speaking School and work personally with Mike Acker:

| **1-on-1 Coaching** | **Professional Online Course Curriculum** | **Monthly Mastermind Cohort** |

Create Confidence through Communication.

1. Overcome insecurity and anxiety.
2. Learn how to connect with others.
3. Develop Executive Presence.

Don't wait: set up a free consultation:
https://advance.as.me/SWNF

(Available for individuals and teams)

ALSO BY MIKE ACKER

A   Lead with No Fear

In this conversational and action-oriented book, Steve Gutzler and Mike Acker present seven shifts to direct your leadership towards your desired destination: impact, influence, and inspiration.

B   Speak with No Fear

Speak With No Fear is the #1 globally highest-ranked book on overcoming the fear of speaking. Full of relatable anecdotes, executable tips, and plenty of laugh-out-loud moments, this book promises to teach you seven proven strategies to help you find your inner presenter.

C   Speak with Confidence

Don't just overcome nervousness; discover Mike Acker's proven framework for developing profound confidence to eliminate self-doubt, second-guessing, and weak presence to excel in public speaking and succeed in life.

D Write to Speak
A simple guide to creating content that connects you with your audience. Readers will learn a repeatable system that works for novice and experienced speakers.

E Connect through Emotional Intelligence
In *Connect through Emotional Intelligence*, you will learn to master yourself, avoid disconnection with others, and bridge gaps through increasing your understanding and applying new principles. Increasing your emotional intelligence will improve your relationships, your leadership, and your life.

BOOK MIKE ACKER

FOR YOUR TEAM OR EVENT

Mike Acker is an in-demand keynote speaker on effective communication, emotional intelligence, and transformational leadership. His work in coaching, writing, and speaking inspires audiences around the nation and the globe. His first book, Speak With No Fear, achieved the status of the highest-ranking book on overcoming nervousness in speaking.

He has worked with Adobe, Amazon, Microsoft, Oracle, INOApps, Dallas International School, US Federal Agencies, International Monetary Fund, and many others.

If you are interested in booking Mike Acker for a keynote presentation, workshop, or virtual program, please contact info@mikeacker.com or visit www.MikeAcker.com.

Past Engagements Include:

WANT TO SUPPORT EFFECTIVE VIRTUAL MEETINGS ACROSS YOUR ORGANIZATION?

Build your Coaching Skills with
Mike's Train-the-Trainer Half-Day Workshop.

A four-hour online or onsite workshop that will transform the way you prepare your team to work from home.

Who it's For: Leaders who want to create a culture of engaged, productive, and enjoyable virtual meetings for their teams.

What We'll Do: Working through *Speak & Meet Virtually* with Mike Acker, the trainer-in-training will discover how to:
- Transform virtual conferencing into engaging and productive meetings.
- Embed the principles of the book into your team's everyday life.
- Change any home office into a professional environment conducive for virtual work.
- Create systems to minimize the waste of time (and money).

With the workshop and the training manual you will learn what to say, how to coach, and what exercises to use in order to embed the principles of the coaching into the culture of the company.

Decrease distractions   **Increase Productivity**   **Amplify Your Results**

Register today at
https://advance.as.me/TRAINER

Made in the USA
Columbia, SC
16 November 2021

49129654R00126